READING AND WRITING Sourcebook

Authors

Robert Pavlik

Richard G. Ramsey

Great Source Education Group

a Houghton Mifflin Company
Wilmington, Massachusetts
www.greatsource.com

Authors

Richard G. Ramsey is currently a national educational consultant for many schools throughout the country and serves as President of Ramsey's Communications. For more than twenty-three years he has served as a teacher and a principal for grades 1–12. Dr. Ramsey has also served on the Curriculum Frameworks Committee for the State of Florida. A lifelong teacher and educator and former principal, he is now a nationally known speaker on improving student achievement and motivating students.

Robert Pavlik taught high school English and reading for seven years. His university assignments in Colorado and Wisconsin have included teaching secondary/content area reading, chairing a Reading/Language Arts Department, and directing a Reading/Learning Center. He is an author of several books and articles and serves as the Director of the School Design and Development Center at Marquette University.

Printed in the United States of America.

International Standard Book Number: 0-669-47137-2

1 2 3 4 5 6 7 8 9 10 — BA — 06 05 04 03 02 01 00

Table of Contents

4

READING AND WRITING Sourcebook

Responding to Literature

What's the secret of understanding what you read? One secret surely is to get involved, to get a pen in your hand and mark up the text. Mark parts that you like, ones you'd like to reread, and even ones you don't understand. Write your questions down. Make predictions about what might happen next. Be sure also to write down how what you are reading connects to <u>your</u> life.

Read this brief poem. The passage has been marked up by a reader to illustrate a variety of response strategies.

RESPONSE NOTES

#71 "No longer mourn for me when I am dead"
by William Shakespeare

No longer mourn for me when I am dead   **1. MARK**
Than you shall hear the (surly sullen bell)   rhyme
Give warning to the world that I am fled
From this <u>vile</u> world, with vilest worms to dwell:
Nay, if you read this line, remember not
The hand that <u>writ</u> it; for I love you so,
That I in your sweet thoughts would be forgot,
If thinking on me then should make you woe.
Oh, if, (I say,) you look upon this verse
When I (perhaps) <u>compounded</u> am with clay,
Do not so much as my poor name rehearse,
But let your love even with my life decay;
    Lest the wise world should look into your moan,
    And <u>mock</u> you with me after I am gone.

2. QUESTION
Why is it a vile world?

3. CLARIFY
writ=wrote

4. VISUALIZE
sullen bell

5. PREDICT
I think this will be a long poem.

6. REACT
a surprise ending

VOCABULARY
surly sullen bell—church bell that sounds to tell everyone someone died.
vile—very bad.
writ—wrote.
compounded—mixed or combined.
mock—laugh at; make fun of.

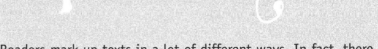

Readers mark up texts in a lot of different ways. In fact, there is no right way or wrong way to do it. Here are 6 general ways readers respond to texts.

1. Mark or Highlight
With a pen, underline or circle words that are important or seem confusing. With a colorful marker, go over parts of a reading. By marking part of a text, you set off important ideas and make them easier to find.

2. Question
Form questions as you read. Ask questions such as, "Do I do this?" and ask questions of the author such as, "Is this true?" This is a way of talking with the author. It triggers thoughts in your mind and makes the reading more meaningful.

3. Clarify
"What does this mean?" You probably ask that question as you read. We try to make clear to ourselves what we have read. Often we will write out a thought in our own words—for example, "This means very bad." Other times we might number or label parts of a text to keep track of events in the plot, arguments an author is making, or connections from one page to another.

4. Visualize
When you read, you see mental pictures of what the writer is describing. To help remember these mental pictures, you can also draw what you see. You can make a chart or organizer or draw a picture or sketch. All of these ways of visualizing are useful.

5. Predict
Another common way of responding to literature is to guess what will happen next. "How will this story come out in the end?" "What will happen next?" Readers make predictions as they read. It is a way of keeping interest in a selection.

6. React and Connect
Readers often write their own opinions or ideas in the margins of books. This, too, is a way of getting more from your reading. It helps you relate what you read to your own life and make sense of it.

Use the response strategies in the Response Notes space beside each selection in this *Sourcebook*. Look back at these examples whenever you need to. Now practice using some of the strategies yourself. Mark up the speech below any way you want. Try to use at least 2 or 3 of the strategies.

"I have the heart and stomach of a king"
by Queen Elizabeth I

RESPONSE NOTES

My loving people, we have been persuaded by some that are careful of our safety, to take heed how we commit ourselves to <u>armed multitudes</u>, for fear of <u>treachery</u>. But I assure you, I do not desire to live to distrust my faithful and loving people. Let <u>tyrants</u> fear . . . I have always so behaved myself that, under God, I have placed my chiefest strength and safeguard in the loyal hearts and good will of my subjects, and therefore I am come amongst you as you see at this time, not for my recreation and <u>disport</u>, but being resolved, in the midst and heat of battle, to live or die amongst you all, to lay down for my God, and for my kingdom, and for my people, my honor and my blood, even in the dust. I know I have the body of a weak and feeble woman, but I have the heart and stomach of a king, and of a king of England too, and think foul scorn that Parma [Italy] or Spain or any Prince of Europe should dare to invade the borders of my realm, to which, rather than any dishonor shall grow by me, I myself will take up arms, I myself will be your general, judge and rewarder of every one of your virtues in the field. I know already for your forwardness you have deserved rewards and crowns, and we do assure you, in the word of a Prince, they shall be duly paid you. . . By your <u>valor</u> in the field, we shall shortly have a famous victory over these enemies of my God, of my kingdom and of my people.

VOCABULARY
armed multitudes—many people who are ready for war.
treachery—deceit or unfaithful behavior.
tyrants—rulers who use power unjustly and cruelly.
disport—amusement.
valor—bravery.

Meeting the Unknown

To the early explorers, much of the world lay clouded in mystery. It was up to adventurers to brave the unpredictable seas and meet the unknown.

Daniel Defoe

Have you ever thought to yourself, "Wow, this looks hard" but then found it was easier than you thought? Many things—including reading—can look too tough to tackle until you take them one step at a time.

BEFORE YOU READ

Take the first step by examining the beginning of *Gulliver's Travels*. Get in a small group and choose a reader.

1. Have the reader read the title and opening paragraph.
2. Then complete the Listener's Guide.

"Shipwreck" *from Gulliver's Travels* by Jonathan Swift

After three years expectation that things would mend, I accepted an <u>advantageous</u> offer from Captain William Prichard, master of the *Antelope*, who was making a voyage to the <u>South-Sea</u>. We set sail from Bristol May 4, 1699, and our voyage at first was very <u>prosperous.</u>

VOCABULARY
advantageous—profitable.
South-Sea—South Pacific Ocean, located south of the equator.
prosperous—successful.

Listener's Guide

Selection title:

What I already know about this story:

Words or phrases I noticed:

(circle one)
I predict this story will be interesting / dull.

(circle one)
I think this story will be easy / hard to understand.

READ

Listen as someone reads the excerpt from *Gulliver's Travels*.
1. **Highlight** anything you think is interesting.
2. Make notes about what puzzles or confuses you.

"Shipwreck" continued

It would not be proper, for some reasons, to trouble the reader with the particulars of our adventures in those seas: let it <u>suffice</u> to inform him, that in our passage from thence to the <u>East Indies</u>, we were driven by a violent storm to the northwest of Van Diemen's Land. By an observation, we found ourselves in the <u>latitude</u> of 30 degrees 2 minutes south. Twelve of our crew were dead by <u>immoderate</u> labor and ill food, the rest were in a very weak condition. On the fifth of November, which was the beginning of summer in those parts, the weather being very hazy, the seamen <u>spied</u> a rock, within half a cable's length of the ship; but the wind was so strong, that we were driven directly upon it, and immediately split.

Response Notes

EXAMPLE:
Strange that reader shouldn't be told the details.

stop+clarify

What happened to the ship the <u>Antelope</u>?

....

....

....

....

stop+clarify

VOCABULARY
suffice—be enough.
East Indies—region that refers to Southeast Asia.
latitude—distance north or south of the equator measured in degrees.
immoderate—extreme; too much.
spied—saw.

stop+predict

What do you predict Gulliver will do now?

....

....

....

....

Response Notes

"Shipwreck" continued

Six of the crew, of whom I was one, having let down the boat into the sea, made a shift to get clear of the ship, and the rock. We rowed by my <u>computation</u> about three <u>leagues</u>, till we were able to work no longer, being already <u>spent</u> with labor while we were in the ship. We therefore trusted ourselves to the mercy of the waves, and in about half an hour the boat was overset by a sudden <u>flurry</u> from the north. What became of my companions in the boat, as well as of those who escaped on the rock, or were left in the <u>vessel</u>, I cannot tell; but conclude they were all lost. For my own part, I swam as fortune directed me, and was pushed forward by wind and tide. I often let my legs drop, and could feel no bottom: but when I was almost gone, and able to struggle no longer, I found myself within my depth; and by this time the storm was much <u>abated</u>. The <u>declivity</u> was so small, that I walked near a mile before I got to the shore, which I <u>conjectured</u>, was about eight o'clock in the evening.

VOCABULARY
computation—adding and subtracting.
leagues—units of distance. In this case, three leagues equals approximately three miles.
spent—exhausted.
flurry—gust of wind.
vessel—small ship.
abated—weaker.
declivity—downward slope.
conjectured—guessed.

stop+question

Why is Gulliver saved—because of luck, skill, or a little of both?

....

....

"Shipwreck" continued

Response Notes

I then advanced forward near half a mile, but could not discover any sign of houses or <u>inhabitants</u>; at least I was in so weak a condition, that I did not observe them. I was extremely tired, and with that, and the heat of the weather, and about half a pint of brandy that I drank as I left the ship, I found myself much <u>inclined</u> to sleep, I lay down on the grass, which was very short and soft, where I slept sounder than ever I remember to have done in my life, and, as I reckoned, above nine hours; for when I awakened, it was just daylight. I attempted to rise, but was not able to stir: for, as I happened to lie on my back, I found my arms and legs were strongly fastened on each side to the ground; and my hair, which was long and thick, tied down in the same manner. I likewise felt several slender <u>ligatures</u> across my body, from my armpits to my thighs. I could only look upwards; the sun began to grow hot, and the light offended my eyes. I heard a confused noise about me, but in the posture I lay, could see nothing except the sky. In a little time I felt something alive moving on my left leg, which advancing gently forward over my breast, came almost up to my chin; when bending my eyes downwards as much as I could, I perceived it to be a human creature not six inches high, with a bow and arrow in his hands, and a <u>quiver</u> at his back. In the meantime, I felt

VOCABULARY
inhabitants—residents.
inclined—in the mood.
ligatures—rope or wires.
quiver—case for holding arrows.

"Shipwreck" continued

at least forty more of the same kind (as I conjectured) following the first. I was in the utmost astonishment, and roared so loud, that they all ran back in a fright; and some of them, as I was afterwards told, were hurt with the falls they got by leaping from my sides upon the ground. However, they soon returned, and one of them, who ventured so far as to get a full sight of my face, lifting up his hands and eyes by way of admiration, cried out in a shrill but distinct voice, *Hekinah degul*: the others repeated the same words several times, but I then knew not what they meant.

stop+question

What question do you have at this point in the story?

....

....

....

stop+question

I lay all this while, as the reader may believe, in great uneasiness: at length, struggling to get loose, I had the fortune to break the strings, and wrench out the pegs that fastened my left arm to the ground; for, by lifting it up to my face, I discovered the methods they had taken to bind me, and at the same time, with a violent pull, which gave me excessive pain, I a little loosened the strings that tied down my hair on the left side, so that I was just able to turn my head about two inches. But the creatures ran off a second time, before I could seize

VOCABULARY
astonishment—state of amazement; shock.
shrill—high-pitched.
bind—tie; restrain.
excessive—great; a large amount of.

"Shipwreck" continued

them; whereupon there was a great shout in a very shrill accent, and after it ceased, I heard one of them cry aloud, *Tolgo phonac;* when in an instant I felt above a hundred arrows discharged on my left hand, which pricked me like so many needles; and besides they shot another flight into the air, as we do bombs in Europe, whereof many, I suppose, fell on my body (though I felt them not) and some on my face, which I immediately covered with my left hand.

When this shower of arrows was over, I fell a groaning with grief and pain, and then striving again to get loose, they discharged another volley larger than the first, and some of them attempted with spears to stick me in the sides; but, by good luck, I had on me a buff jerkin, which they could not pierce. I thought it the most prudent method to lie still, and my design was to continue so till night, when, my left hand being already loose, I could easily free myself: and as for the inhabitants, I had reason to believe I might be a match for the greatest armies they could bring against me, if they were all of the same size with him that I saw.

▼ VOCABULARY ▬
striving—struggling.
volley—shower of stones, bullets, or arrows.
buff jerkin—military uniform coat made of the thick skin of a buffalo.
prudent—wise.
design—plan.

stop+summarize

What were some of the difficulties Gulliver had to face?

....

....

....

....

....

....

III GATHER YOUR THOUGHTS

A. NARROW THE FOCUS When you narrow the focus of your writing, you take a big topic (A Big Adventure) and divide it into smaller subtopics.

1. Practice narrowing a topic of your own.

2. Start with "My Biggest Adventure." Then narrow the topic into a smaller one to write about.

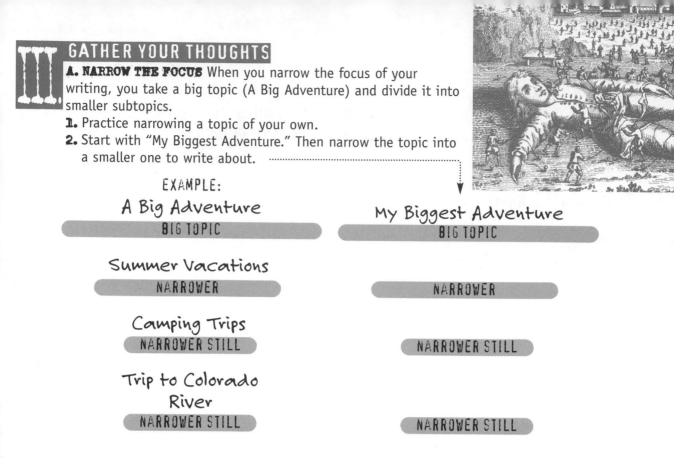

EXAMPLE:

A Big Adventure

BIG TOPIC

My Biggest Adventure

BIG TOPIC

Summer Vacations

NARROWER

NARROWER

Camping Trips

NARROWER STILL

NARROWER STILL

Trip to Colorado River

NARROWER STILL

NARROWER STILL

B. DEVELOP AND SUPPORT A TOPIC SENTENCE Now prepare to write a paragraph about the narrowed topic you listed above.

1. Start by writing a topic sentence. This will be your main idea.

2. Then think of 3 details that support the topic sentence.

MY TOPIC: Trip to Colorado River

TOPIC SENTENCE: My trip to the Colorado River was a major adventure.

DETAIL #1 camping on the Colorado

DETAIL #2 tipping the raft over in the Colorado River

DETAIL #3 long hike out of the canyon

My topic:

Topic sentence:

My details:

1.

2.

3.

IV. WRITE

Write a **paragraph** about an adventure you have had.

1. Begin with a topic sentence.
2. Add 3-4 detail sentences that describe your adventure.
3. End with a concluding sentence that explains how your adventure ended.
4. Use the Writers' Checklist to help you revise your paragraph.

WRITERS' CHECKLIST

SENTENCES

☐ Did you always begin with a capital letter?

☐ Did you always end with a punctuation mark?

☐ Did you express a complete thought in each sentence?

EXAMPLE: My adventure started at the top of the canyon.

V. WRAP-UP

What made the excerpt from *Gulliver's Travels* easy or difficult to read?

2:

When you read, do you ever ask yourself, "What if I were this character? What would I say? How would I solve this problem?" These kinds of questions can help you connect to what you are reading.

I. BEFORE YOU READ

Robinson Crusoe is a novel about a man shipwrecked on an island.
1. Read the 3 questions below.
2. Decide which question interests you the most.
3. Quickwrite an answer to the question for 1 minute.

Question #1
What would you do first if you were shipwrecked on a deserted island?

Question #2
Would you risk your life to save the life of someone you didn't know?

Question #3
How can you tell if someone is a coward or a hero?

1-Minute Quickwrite

QUESTION # ___

Read the excerpt from *Robinson Crusoe*.
1. Keep track of the story's events. Each time something new happens, make a note in the Response Notes.
2. Try to **visualize** the events by mapping or sketching the scene.

Response Notes

EXAMPLE:

Canoes
discovered.

"Visitors" from *Robinson Crusoe* by Daniel Defoe

I was surprised one morning early, with seeing no less than five canoes all on shore together on my side of the island; and the people who belonged to them all landed, and out of my sight. The number of them broke all my measures, for seeing so many, and knowing that they always came four or six, or sometimes more in a boat, I could not tell what to think of it, or how to take my measures to attack twenty or thirty men single handed; so I lay still in my castle, perplexed and discomforted; however, I put myself into all the same postures for an attack that I had formerly provided, and was just ready for action, if anything had presented.

stop+visualize

What does the scene look like? Draw a map.

VOCABULARY
perplexed and discomforted—troubled; confused.
postures—positions.

"Visitors" continued

Having waited a good while, listening to hear if they made any noise, at length, being very impatient, I set my guns at the foot of my ladder, and <u>clambered</u> up to the top of the hill, by my two stages as usual; standing so, however, that my head did not appear above the hill, so that they could not perceive me by any means; here I observed, by the help of my <u>perspective glass</u>, that they were no less than thirty in number, that they had a fire <u>kindled</u>, that they had had meat <u>dressed</u>. How they cooked it, that I knew not, or what it was; but they were all dancing in I know not how many <u>barbarous</u> gestures and figures, their own way, round the fire.

While I was thus looking on them, I perceived by my perspective two miserable <u>wretches</u> dragged from the boats, where it seems they were laid by, and were now brought out for the <u>slaughter</u>. I perceived one of them immediately fell, being knocked down, I suppose with a club or wooden sword, for that was their way, and two or three others were at work immediately cutting him open for their cookery, while the other victim was left standing by himself, till they should be ready for him.

stop+organize

What has happened so far? Record the events in the graphic organizer below.

```
┌────────────────┐          ┌────────────────┐
│                │  ● ● ● ►  │                │
│                │          │                │
└────────────────┘          └────────────────┘
```

VOCABULARY
clambered—climbed with difficulty.
perspective glass—instrument similar to a telescope or binoculars.
kindled—lit.
dressed—prepared.
barbarous—savage; uncivilized.
wretches—mean people.
slaughter—mass killing.

In that very moment this poor wretch seeing himself a little at liberty, nature inspired him with hopes of life, and he started away from them, and ran with incredible swiftness along the sands directly towards me, I mean towards that part of the coast where my <u>habitation</u> was.

I was dreadfully frighted (that I must acknowledge) when I perceived him to run my way, and especially when, as I thought, I saw him pursued by the whole body; and now I expected that part of my dream was coming to pass, and that he would certainly take shelter in my <u>grove</u>; but I could not depend by any means upon my dream for the rest of it, viz. that the other <u>savages</u> would not pursue him <u>thither</u>, and find him there. However, I kept my station, and my spirits began to recover when I found that there was not above three men that followed him, and still more was I encouraged when I found that he outstrip'd them exceedingly in running, and gained ground of them, so that if he could but hold it for half an hour, I saw easily he would fairly get away from them all.

There was between them and my castle the creek which I mentioned often at the first part of my story, when I landed my cargoes out of the ship; and this, I saw plainly, he must necessarily swim over, or the poor wretch would be taken there.

stop+organize

What other events have happened? Add 2 more events to the graphic organizer.

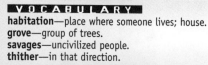

VOCABULARY
habitation—place where someone lives; house.
grove—group of trees.
savages—uncivilized people.
thither—in that direction.

"Visitors" continued

But when the savage escaping came thither, he made nothing of it, tho' the tide was then up, but plunging in, swam thro' in about thirty strokes or thereabouts, landed, and ran on with exceeding strength and swiftness; when the three persons came to the creek, I found that two of them could swim, but the third could not, and that standing on the other side, he looked at the other, but went no further, and soon after went softly back again, which, as it happened, was very well for him in the main.

I observed that the two who swam were yet more than twice as long swimming over the creek as the fellow was that fled from them. It came now very warmly upon my thoughts, and indeed irresistibly, that now was my time to get me a servant, and perhaps a companion or assistant; and that I was called plainly by <u>Providence</u> to save this poor creature's life; I immediately run down the ladders with all possible <u>expedition</u>, fetched my two guns, for they were both but at the foot of the ladders, as I observed above; and getting up again, with the same <u>haste</u>, to the top of the hill, I crossed toward the sea; and having a very short cut, and all down hill, clapped myself in the way between the pursuers and the pursued; <u>hallowing</u>

stop+organize

What other events have happened? Record at least 2 more things that have happened.

VOCABULARY
Providence—God.
expedition—speed.
haste—quickness.
hallowing—calling.

"Visitors" continued

aloud to him that fled, who looking back, was at first perhaps as much frighted at me as at them; but I <u>beckoned</u> with my hand to him to come back; and in the mean time, I slowly advanced towards the two that followed; then rushing at once upon the <u>foremost</u>, I knocked him down with the <u>stock of my piece</u>; I was <u>loath</u> to fire, because I would not have the rest hear; though at that distance it would not have been easily heard, and being out of sight of the smoke too, they would not have easily known what to make of it. Having knocked this fellow down, the other who pursued with him stopped, as if he had been frighted; and I advanced <u>apace</u> towards him; but as I came nearer, I perceived presently he had a bow and arrow, and was fitting it to shoot at me; so I was then necessitated to shoot at him first, which I did, and killed him at the first shoot; the poor savage who fled, but had stopped, though he saw both his enemies fallen and killed, as he thought, yet was so frighted with the fire and noise of my piece, that he stood <u>stock still</u>, and neither came forward or went backward, tho' he seemed rather <u>inclined</u> to fly still than to come on; I hallowed again to him, and made signs to come forward, which he easily understood, and came a little way, then stopped again, and then a little further, and

stop+organize

What other events have happened? Record at least 2 more things that have happened.

VOCABULARY
beckoned—motioned.
foremost—nearest.
stock of my piece—rear handle of my weapon.
loath—reluctant; not wanting.
apace—swiftly.
stock still—unmoving.
inclined—in the mood.

"Visitors" continued

stopped again, and I could then perceive that he stood trembling, as if he had been taken prisoner, and had just been to be killed, as his two enemies were. I beckoned him again to come to me, and gave him all the signs of encouragement that I could think of, and he came nearer and nearer, kneeling down every ten or twelve steps in token of acknowledgment for my saving his life. I smiled at him, and looked pleasantly, and beckoned to him to come still nearer; at length he came close to me, and then he kneeled down again, kissed the ground, and laid his head upon the ground, and taking me by the foot, set my foot upon his head; this it seems was in token of swearing to be my slave for ever; I took him up, and made much of him, and encouraged him all I could.

stop+reflect

Recall what has happened in the entire story. Then use the Story String below to record the major events in the story's beginning, middle, and end.

Story String

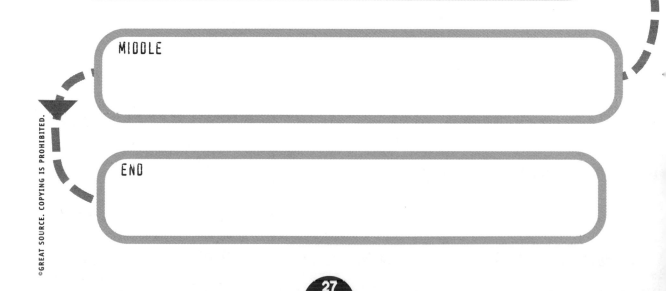

BEGINNING

MIDDLE

END

GATHER YOUR THOUGHTS

A. PLAN A NARRATIVE A narrative tells a story and has a beginning, middle, and end.

1. Look at the chart showing the story of *Robinson Crusoe*.

2. Then think about an experience from your own life that you could write about. Describe the "story" in the chart. ┄┄┄┄┄┄┄┄

EXAMPLE:

BEGINNING	MIDDLE	END
1. Strangers land on island.	**2.** Captive runs away.	**3.** Crusoe helps save the captive.

BEGINNING	MIDDLE	END
1.	**2.**	**3.**

B. DEVELOP THE NARRATIVE Create a quick list of things that happen in your story. Write for 1 minute, jotting down a list of events and people in your story.

1. _____
2. _____
3. _____
4. _____

5. _____
6. _____
7. _____
8. _____

C. PLAN THE BEGINNING AND ENDING The key to a good story is how it is told, especially how it begins and ends. Complete the organizer below to help you begin and end your narrative. Start with the middle box.

BEGINNING SENTENCE	What is the most important event?	ENDING SENTENCE
What comes right before the event?		What comes after the event?

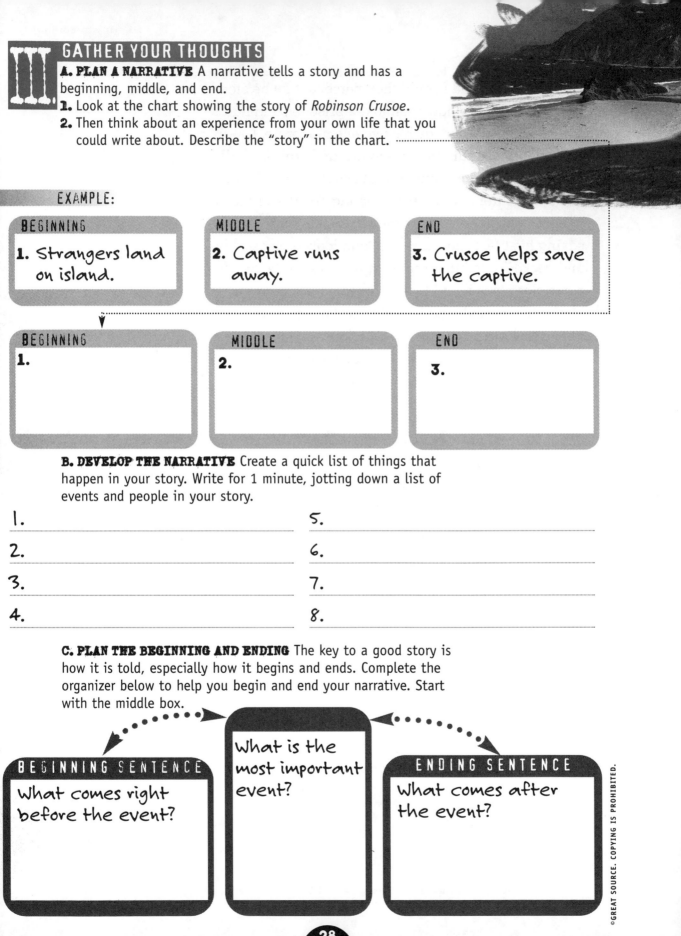

IV. WRITE

Now write a **narrative paragraph** about your experience.

1. Start with the beginning sentence from the previous page.

2. Then develop the middle of your paragraph, telling about the most important part of the experience.

3. End the narrative shortly after that.

4. Use the Writers' Checklist to help you revise.

WRITERS' CHECKLIST

COMMAS

Commas can keep words and ideas from running together.

❑ Did you use a comma to separate items in a series? EXAMPLE: Find a bucket, a shovel, and some sand.

❑ in dates and addresses? EXAMPLE: Let's visit Houston, Texas.

❑ in numbers of four digits or more? EXAMPLE: 1,000,000.

❑ to set off interruptions? EXAMPLE: Sir, I command you to halt!

❑ between two independent clauses that are joined by and, but, or, nor, for, so, or yet? EXAMPLE: My ship is ready to sail, but my crew has not arrived.

V. WRAP-UP

What part of *Robinson Crusoe* did you like reading about?

Land and Rivers

Land and Rivers

Geographical features—such as rolling hills, lush valleys, and winding rivers—can inspire us with their beauty. They affect how we live and work and give a certain shape to our lives.

AFRICA

Do you ever dream about faraway lands? Have you ever wanted to travel around the world? Reading lets you go anywhere any time. In this story, Joseph Conrad tells a tale about the love of travel.

BEFORE YOU READ

Gather your thoughts about travel before you begin. Think about what travel means to you. Then complete the Word Web.

1. Write your ideas about travel on the arms of the web. Add as many ideas as you can.

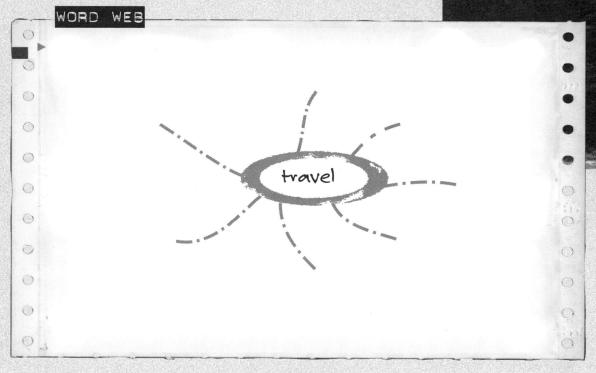

WORD WEB

travel

2. Then make a prediction about this selection.

What do you think a selection called "The River" will say about travel?

READ

Now read about the idea of travel in this excerpt entitled "The River."

1. As you read, **mark** or **highlight** parts that interest you.

2. Think about how the story connects to your own ideas about travel.

"The River" from *Heart of Darkness*
by Joseph Conrad

RESPONSE NOTES

"I don't want to bother you much with what happened to me personally," he began, showing in this remark the weakness of many tellers of tales who seem so often unaware of what their <u>audience</u> would best like to hear; "yet to understand the effect of it on me you ought to know how I got out there, what I saw, how I went up that river to the place where I first met the poor chap. It was the farthest point of <u>navigation</u> and the <u>culminating</u> point of my experience. It seemed somehow to throw a kind of light on everything about me—and into my thoughts. It was <u>somber</u> enough too—and pitiful—not extraordinary in all way—not very clear either. No, not very clear. And yet it seemed to throw a kind of light.

EXAMPLE:
Yes, people love to give too many details in their stories.

stop and retell

What is happening so far?

_____

_____

_____

VOCABULARY
audience—listeners.
navigation—travel by ship.
culminationg—final or last.
somber—serious.

RESPONSE NOTES

"I had then, as you remember, just returned to London after a lot of Indian Ocean, Pacific, China Seas— a regular <u>dose</u> of the East—six years or so, and I was loafing about, hindering you fellows in your work and invading your homes, just as though I had got a heavenly mission to <u>civilize</u> you. It was very fine for a time, but after a bit I did get tired of resting. Then I began to look for a ship—I should think the hardest work on earth. But the ships wouldn't even look at me. And I got tired of that game too.

"Now when I was a little chap I had a <u>passion</u> for maps. I would look for hours at South America, or Africa, or Australia, and lose myself in all the glories of exploration. At that time there were many blank spaces on the earth, and when I saw one that looked particularly inviting on a map (but they all look that) I would put my finger on it and say, When I grow up I will go there. The North Pole was one of these places, I remember. Well, I haven't been there yet, and shall not try now. The glamour's off. Other places were scattered about the <u>Equator</u>, and in every sort of <u>latitude</u> all over the two <u>hemispheres</u>. I have been in some of them, and . . . well, we won't talk about that. But there was one yet—the biggest, the most blank, so to speak—that I had a <u>hankering</u> after.

stop and retell

What is the man explaining?

_____

_____

_____

VOCABULARY

dose—amount of an unpleasant experience.
civilize—improve; refine.
passion—enthusiasm; love.
Equator—imaginary circle around the earth that is the boundary between the Northern and Southern Hemispheres.
latitude—distance from the equator.
hemispheres—northern or southern halves of the earth's surface.
hankering—desire; craving.

"The River" CONTINUED

"True, by this time it was not a blank space any more. It had got filled since my boyhood with rivers and lakes and names. It had ceased to be a blank space of delightful mystery—a white patch for a boy to dream gloriously over. It had become a place of darkness. But there was in it one river especially, a mighty big river, that you could see on the map, resembling an <u>immense</u> snake uncoiled, with its head in the sea, its body at rest curving afar over a vast country, and its tail lost in the depths of the land. And as I looked at the map of it in a shop-window, it fascinated me as a snake would a bird—a silly little bird. Then I remembered there was a big <u>concern</u>, a Company for trade on that river. Dash it all! I thought to myself, they can't trade without using some kind of craft on that lot of fresh water—steamboats! Why shouldn't I try to get charge of one? I went on along <u>Fleet Street</u>, but could not shake off the idea. The snake had charmed me.

stop and retell

What does the man think of the river?

_____

_____

_____

_____

VOCABULARY
immense—huge.
concern—business or company. *Heart of Darkness* describes the business of ivory trading along the Congo, a river in central Africa.
Fleet Street—business district in London, England.

GATHER YOUR THOUGHTS

A. BRAINSTORM SUBJECT IDEAS The main idea is the most important idea in an expository paragraph. Usually it comes in the topic sentence of a paragraph.

1. Brainstorm ideas on travel you might want to write about in a paragraph.

BRAINSTORM

2. Narrow the larger, general idea into 3 smaller subjects. List several points you could make about each.

Travel

3. Then choose 1 subject and write a topic sentence about it.

TOPIC SENTENCE:

B. DEVELOP A MAIN IDEA Writers need to support the main idea with details.

1. Write your main idea, or topic sentence, in the box at the top.

2. Add 3-4 detail sentences about that idea.

3. Write a closing sentence that restates your main idea.

MAIN IDEA:

DETAIL:

DETAIL:

DETAIL:

DETAIL:

CLOSING SENTENCE:

WRITE

Now write your ideas about travel in an **expository paragraph**.

1. Start with your main idea in a topic sentence.
2. Support your main idea with details from your organizer and end with a closing sentence that restates your main idea in an interesting way.
3. Use the Writers' Checklist to help you revise.

WRITERS' CHECKLIST

SUBJECT/VERB AGREEMENT

☐ **Did the subject and verbs in your sentences agree? A singular subject takes a singular verb, and a plural subject takes a plural verb.**
EXAMPLES: *The idea of travel is exciting. (singular) The ideas seem intelligent ones. (plural)*

☐ **Did all of your sentences with compound subjects agree?**
EXAMPLE: *The suitcase and bag were onboard the ship. (plural subject)*

V. WRAP-UP

In your opinion, what is this selection by Joseph Conrad about?

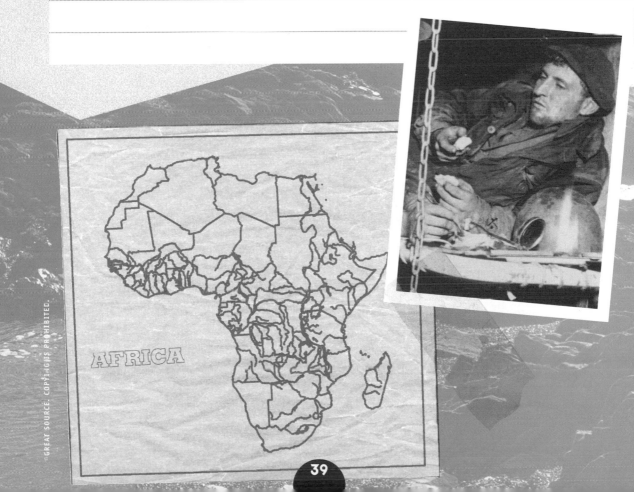

AFRICA

4 : The Land

What places do you love? In the novel *Cry, the Beloved Country,* Alan Paton describes the land and what it seemed like for some people in South Africa. In this beginning of the novel, Paton describes two different views of the South African countryside.

I. BEFORE YOU READ

Look at the organizer below. Read the headings.

1. Skim the reading to find details about the land described.

2. Fill out the organizer with details you noticed while skimming.

PLACE NAMES

NEW, UNUSUAL WORDS

THINGS DESCRIBED

READ

Read the selection carefully and at your own pace.
1. In the Response Notes, **react** and **connect** by writing your own ideas and comments about Paton's description.
2. Note any descriptive words and details that stand out for you.

"The Land" from *Cry, the Beloved Country* by Alan Paton

There is a lovely road that runs from Ixopo into the hills. These hills are grass-covered and rolling, and they are lovely beyond any singing of it. The road climbs seven miles into them, to Carisbrooke; and from there, if there is no mist, you look down on one of the fairest valleys of Africa. About you there is grass and <u>bracken</u> and you may hear the <u>forlorn</u> crying of the titihoya, one of the birds of the <u>veld</u>. Below you is the valley of the Umzimkulu, on its journey from the Drakensberg to the sea; and beyond and behind the river, great hill after great hill; and beyond and behind them, the mountains of Ingeli and East Griqualand.

stop and think

What feeling is created by this description?

_____

_____

_____

RESPONSE NOTES

EXAMPLE:
The beach is a lovely place for me.

VOCABULARY
bracken—kind of green plant; fern.
forlorn—sad and lonely.
veld—open grazing areas of South Africa.

RESPONSE NOTES

The grass is rich and <u>matted</u>, you cannot see the soil. It holds the rain and the mist, and they seep into the ground, feeding the streams in every <u>kloof</u>. It is <u>well-tended</u>, and not too many cattle feed upon it; not too many fires burn it, laying bare the soil. Stand <u>unshod</u> upon it, for the ground is holy, being even as it came from the <u>Creator</u>. Keep it, guard it, care for it, for it keeps men, guards men, cares for men. Destroy it and man is destroyed.

stop and think

What is Paton saying about the land?

....

....

....

....

....

....

....

....

VOCABULARY
matted—dense; tangled together.
kloof—long, deep narrow valley created by running water.
well-tended—well taken care of.
unshod—barefoot.
Creator—superior being believed to have created the earth; God.

"The Land" CONTINUED

Where you stand the grass is rich and matted, you cannot see the soil. But the rich green hills break down. They fall to the valley below, and falling, change their nature. For they grow red and bare; they cannot hold the rain and mist, and the streams are dry in the kloofs. Too many cattle feed upon the grass, and too many fires have burned it. Stand shod upon it, for it is coarse and sharp, and the stones cut under the feet. It is not <u>kept</u>, or guarded, or cared for, it no longer keeps men, guards men, cares for men. The titihoya does not cry here any more.

RESPONSE NOTES

VOCABULARY
kept—neatly maintained.

stop and think

What comparison is Paton making between the land below and the land above?

....

....

....

....

Sketch the scene that Paton is describing.

GATHER YOUR THOUGHTS

A. IDENTIFY DESCRIPTIVE WORDS Think about the description Paton gives of the land.

1. Reread the selection.

2. Make a list of key descriptive words below.

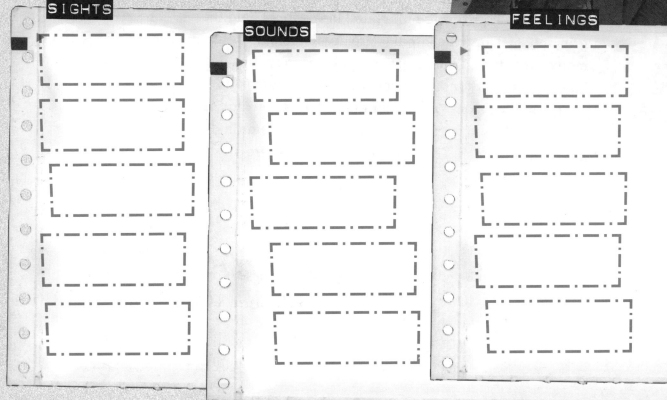

SIGHTS

SOUNDS

FEELINGS

B. REFLECT Now choose a place to describe in a paragraph of your own.

1. Write the name of your place in the center.

2. On the arms of the web, jot down words and experiences that you associate with the place.

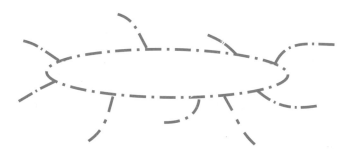

C. ORGANIZE DETAILS Think about the order in which you can best present the details that describe your place.

1. Use your web to help you arrange details in the organizer below.
2. Go back and number the details in the order that would make most sense to use in your description.

SOUNDS

SIGHTS

SMELLS

FEELINGS

EXPERIENCES

IV. WRITE

Write a **descriptive paragraph** of a place. Use your notes to help you.

1. Start with a topic sentence that lets readers know the place you are describing.
2. Then, in an order that makes the most sense, add many sensory details to describe your place.
3. Use the Writers' Checklist to help you revise your paragraph.

WRITERS' CHECKLIST

EASILY CONFUSED WORDS

❏ Did you check to be sure you used *there*, *their*, and *they're* correctly? *There* refers to a place. *Their* shows ownership. *They're* is a contraction that means "they are." EXAMPLES: *There* in the valley Paton sees women working in the fields. *They're* trying to grow corn on ground that is not fertile. *Their* luck is running out.

❏ Did you use *it's* and *its* correctly? *It's* is a contraction that means "it is." *Its* shows ownership. EXAMPLES: *It's* beautiful in the mountains. The ground is rich. *Its* surface is covered with mist.

V. WRAP-UP

What did you learn from reading this selection?

READERS' CHECKLIST

MEANING

☐ Did you learn something from the reading?

☐ Did it affect you or make an impression?

Chinua Achebe

Chinua Achebe (1930-) was born in Nigeria. His poems and novels reflect his country's culture and traditions. *Things Fall Apart* is Achebe's most famous novel. It describes the arrival of Europeans in Nigeria in the 1800s.

Chinua Achebe

THINGS FALL APART

EVERYMAN'S LIBRARY

Who is the most interesting person you know? For many of us, some of the most interesting people are characters in movies or stories. Characters give a story a central point around which things happen and can reveal important clues about the author's message.

BEFORE YOU READ

Choose a partner and read the sentences below from "Okonkwo's Story" to each other.

1. Put a 1 before the sentence that you think comes first in the story, a 2 before the one you think comes next, and so on.
2. Share your answers with other readers.
3. Then use the questions below to discuss what you learned from this look-ahead into the story.

PAIR-AND-SHARE

	"The drums beat and the flutes sang and the spectators held their breath."
	"Unoka, the grown-up, was a failure."
	"He had no patience with his father."
	"Unoka was, of course, a debtor, and he owed every neighbor some money, from a few cowries to quite substantial amounts."

QUESTIONS TO CONSIDER

1. What do you think "Okonkwo's Story," part of the novel Things Fall Apart, is about?

2. What do you predict "falls apart" in the story?

READ

Stay with your partner. Take turns reading the story aloud.
1. As you read, stop along the way to **clarify** what the author is telling you about Okonkwo.
2. Use the Response Notes space to make notes.

"Okonkwo's Story" from *Things Fall Apart*
by Chinua Achebe

Okonkwo was well known throughout the nine villages and even beyond. <u>His fame rested on solid personal achievements</u>. As a young man of eighteen he had brought honor to his village by throwing Amalinze the Cat. Amalinze was the great wrestler who for seven years was unbeaten, from <u>Umuofia</u> to <u>Mbaino</u>. He was called the Cat because his back would never touch the earth. It was this man that Okonkwo threw in a fight which the old men agreed was one of the fiercest since the founder of their town engaged a spirit of the wild for seven days and seven nights.

RESPONSE NOTES

EXAMPLE:
Okonkwo is admired.

READER'S LOG

Say what you think this sentence means:

"... he had brought honor to his village by throwing Amalinze the Cat."

....

....

....

....

....

VOCABULARY
Umuofia, Mbaino—distant villages in Africa.

The drums beat and the flutes sang and the spectators held their breath. Amalinze was a wily craftsman but Okonkwo was as slippery as a fish in water. Every nerve and every muscle stood out on their arms, on their backs and their thighs, and one almost heard them stretching to breaking point. In the end Okonkwo threw the Cat.

That was many years ago, twenty years or more, and during this time Okonkwo's fame had grown like a bush fire in the <u>harmattan</u>. He was tall and huge, and his bushy eyebrows and wide nose gave him a very severe look. He breathed heavily, and it was said that, when he slept, his wives and children in their houses could hear him breathe. When he walked, his heels hardly touched the ground and he seemed to walk on springs, as if he was going to pounce on somebody. And he did pounce on people quite often. He had a slight <u>stammer</u> and whenever he was angry and could not get his words out quickly enough, he would use his fists. He had no patience with unsuccessful men. He had had no patience with his father.

READER'S LOG

What does this sentence mean?

"He had a slight stammer and whenever he was angry and could not get his words out quickly enough, he would use his fists."

READER'S LOG

VOCABULARY
harmattan—dry, dusty, northwest coast of Africa.
stammer—habit of pausing or repeating sounds while speaking.

"Okonkwo's Story" continued

Unoka, for that was his father's name, had died ten years ago. In his day he was lazy and <u>improvident</u> and was quite incapable of thinking about tomorrow. If any money came his way, and it seldom did, he immediately bought gourds of palm-wine, called round his neighbors and <u>made merry</u>. He always said that whenever he saw a dead man's mouth he saw the folly of not eating what one had in one's lifetime. Unoka was, of course, a <u>debtor</u>, and he owed every neighbor some money, from a few <u>cowries</u> to quite substantial amounts.

He was tall but very thin and had a slight <u>stoop</u>. He wore a <u>haggard</u> and <u>mournful</u> look except when he was drinking or playing on his flute. He was very good on his flute, and his happiest moments were the two or three moons after the harvest when the village musicians brought down their instruments, hung above the fireplace.

STOP AND THINK

What 3 adjectives would you use to describe Unoka?

....

....

....

....

....

VOCABULARY
improvident—not cautious of the future.
made merry—celebrated; partied.
debtor—person who owed money.
cowries—units of African currency.
stoop—forward bending of the head and upper back.
haggard—tired.
mournful—sad.

Unoka would play with them, his face beaming with blessedness and peace. Sometimes another village would ask Unoka's band and their dancing *egwugwu* to come and stay with them and teach them their tunes. They would go to such hosts for as long as three or four markets, making music and feasting. Unoka loved the good <u>fare</u> and the good fellowship, and he loved this season of the year, when the rains had stopped and the sun rose every morning with dazzling beauty.

And it was not too hot either, because the cold and dry harmattan wind was blowing down from the north. Some years the harmattan was very severe and a dense haze hung on the atmosphere. Old men and children would then sit round log fires, warming their bodies. Unoka loved it all, and he loved the first <u>kites</u> that returned with the dry season, and the children who sang songs of welcome to them.

STOP AND THINK

Would you say Unoka is a likable person? Why or why not?

....

....

....

....

VOCABULARY
fare—food and drink.
kites—hawk-like birds.

"Okonkwo's Story" continued

He would remember his own childhood, how he had often wandered around looking for a kite sailing <u>leisurely</u> against the blue sky. As soon as he found one, he would sing with his whole being, welcoming it back from its long, long journey, and asking it if it had brought home any lengths of cloth.

That was years ago, when he was young. Unoka, the grown-up, was a failure. He was poor and his wife and children had barely enough to eat. People laughed at him because he was a <u>loafer</u>, and they swore never to lend him any more money because he never paid back. But Unoka was such a man that he always succeeded in borrowing more, and piling up his debts.

READER'S LOG

How does this sentence from the story make you feel? What is Achebe saying about Unoka?

"But Unoka was such a man that he always succeeded in borrowing more, and piling up his debts."

VOCABULARY
leisurely—slowly.
loafer—lazy person.

A. UNDERSTAND DETAILS Writers give details so that readers can feel that they know the characters in a story.

1. Go back through the story again, looking for details about Okonkwo.
2. Fill out the organizer to form a clearer picture of him.

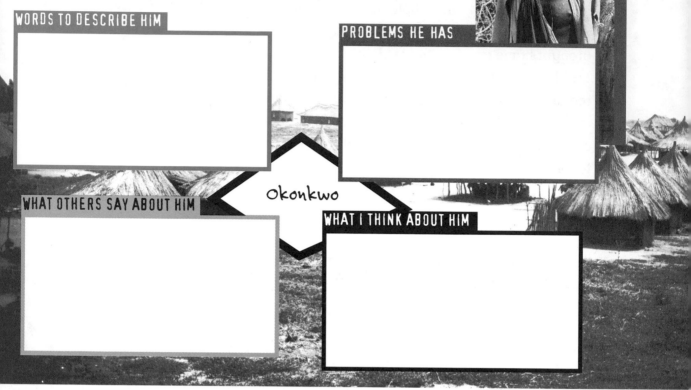

WORDS TO DESCRIBE HIM

PROBLEMS HE HAS

Okonkwo

WHAT OTHERS SAY ABOUT HIM

WHAT I THINK ABOUT HIM

B. DESCRIBE A CHARACTER Now think of an interesting character you know—a real person or a story or movie character—that you could write a story about.

1. Write the name of the person in the center of the cluster.
2. On the lines, write details that describe the character and a problem he or she has.

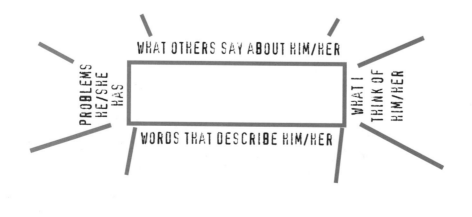

WHAT OTHERS SAY ABOUT HIM/HER

PROBLEMS HE/SHE HAS

WHAT I THINK OF HIM/HER

WORDS THAT DESCRIBE HIM/HER

IV. WRITE

Write a **story beginning** about a person you know who is an interesting character. You will finish your story in the next lesson.

1. Describe the character and an interesting problem he or she has. Use your notes on the previous page to help you get started.

2. Use the Writers' Checklist to help you revise.

Title:

Continue your writing on the next page.

WRITERS' CHECKLIST

COMMAS

☐ **Did you use commas to separate items in a series?** EXAMPLE: *She was smart, pretty, and funny.*

☐ **Did you use commas to separate an appositive (an identifying word or phrase) from the rest of the sentence?** EXAMPLE: *Unoka, a lazy man, refused to work for a living.*

☐ **Did you use commas to introduce a direct quotation?** EXAMPLE: *Okonkwo once said, "Why work when I don't have to?"*

Continue your writing from the previous page.

WRAP-UP

V. What ideas did Achebe's story make you think about?

6: Okonkwo's Story continued

When was the last time a story really surprised you and did *not* turn out the way you thought? You probably remember it. When you make predictions, you take more of an interest in a story.

BEFORE YOU READ

Look back over the first part of "Okonkwo's Story" in the last lesson.

1. With a partner, try to summarize what has happened in the story so far.
2. Fill in the Anticipation/Reaction Guide below.
3. Discuss your predictions with your partner and the rest of the class.

"Okonkwo's Story"

BEFORE READING		AFTER READING	
seems likely	seems unlikely	did happen	did not happen

1. OKONKWO FORGIVES UNOKA FOR HIS LAZY WAYS. ☐ ☐ ☐ ☐

2. UNOKA ASKS HIS SON FOR MONEY TO PAY OFF THE DEBTS. ☐ ☐ ☐ ☐

3. UNOKA DIES A HAPPY MAN. ☐ ☐ ☐ ☐

4. OKONKWO BECOMES A WEALTHY FARMER WITH THREE WIVES AND TWO HONORARY TITLES. ☐ ☐ ☐ ☐

5. OKONKWO REMAINS ASHAMED OF HIS FATHER. ☐ ☐ ☐ ☐

How will the story turn out?

_____

_____

_____

_____

ANTICIPATION/REACTION GUIDE

READ

With your reading partner, take turns reading aloud from the
second part of this excerpt from *Things Fall Apart*.
1. Highlight or **mark** parts that help you know how the story
might turn out.
2. Explain your ideas in the Response Notes.

EXAMPLE:
Sounds like he's
lazy and won't
work hard.

"Okonkwo's Story" (continued) from *Things Fall Apart*
by Chinua Achebe

One day a neighbor called Okoye came in to see
[Unoka]. He was reclining on a mud bed in his hut
playing on the flute. He immediately rose and
shook hands with Okoye, who then unrolled the
goatskin which he carried under his arm, and sat down.
Unoka went into an inner room and soon returned with
a small wooden disc containing a kola nut, some
alligator pepper and a lump of white chalk.

"I have kola," he announced when he sat down, and
passed the disc over to his guest.

"Thank you. He who brings kola brings life. But I
think you ought to break it," replied Okoye, passing
back the disc.

"No, it is for you, I think," and they argued like this
for a few moments before Unoka accepted the honor of
breaking the kola. Okoye, meanwhile, took the lump of
chalk, drew some lines on the floor, and then painted
his big toe.

STOP AND REFLECT

Why does Okoye want Unoka to break the Kola?

STOP AND REFLECT

As he broke the kola, Unoka prayed to their
ancestors for life and health, and for protection against

VOCABULARY
kola nut—kind of food eaten by African people.

"Okonkwo's Story" continued

their enemies. When they had eaten they talked about many things: about the heavy rains which were drowning the yams, about the next ancestral feast and about the <u>impending</u> war with the village of Mbaino. Unoka was never happy when it came to wars. He was in fact a coward and could not bear the sight of blood. And so he changed the subject and talked about music, and his face beamed. He could hear in his mind's ear the blood-stirring and intricate rhythms of the *ekwe* and the *udu* and the *ogene*, and he could hear his own flute weaving in and out of them, decorating them with a colorful and <u>plaintive</u> tune. The total effect was <u>gay</u> and <u>brisk</u>, but if one picked out the flute as it went up and down and then broke up into short snatches, one saw that there was sorrow and grief there.

Okoye was also a musician. He played on the *ogene*. But he was not a failure like Unoka. He had a large barn full of yams and he had three wives. And now he was going to take the Idemili title, the third highest in the land. It was a very expensive ceremony and he was gathering all his <u>resources</u> together. That was in fact the reason why he had come to see Unoka. He cleared his throat and began:

"Thank you for the kola. You may have heard of the title I intend to take shortly."

STOP AND THINK

What does Okoye want from Unoka?

....

....

....

....

STOP AND THINK

VOCABULARY
impending—upcoming.
plaintive—gloomy; sad.
gay—cheerful.
brisk—lively.
resources—money and other belongings.

Having spoken plainly so far, Okoye said the next half a dozen sentences in <u>proverbs</u>. Among the Ibo the art of conversation is regarded very highly, and proverbs are the palm-oil with which words are eaten. Okoye was a great talker and he spoke for a long time, <u>skirting round</u> the subject and then hitting it finally. In short, he was asking Unoka to return the two hundred cowries he had borrowed from him more than two years before. As soon as Unoka understood what his friend was driving at, he burst out laughing. He laughed loud and long and his voice rang out clear as the *ogene*, and tears stood in his eyes. His visitor was amazed, and sat speechless. At the end, Unoka was able to give an answer between fresh outbursts of <u>mirth</u>.

STOP AND THINK

Do you think Unoka will agree to pay back the loan from Okoye? Why or why not?

....

....

....

"Look at that wall," he said, pointing at the far wall of his hut, which was rubbed with red earth so that it shone. "Look at those lines of chalk;" and Okoye saw groups of short <u>perpendicular</u> lines drawn in chalk. There were five

VOCABULARY

proverbs—short, common sayings.
skirting round—avoiding by moving closely around.
mirth—gladness.
perpendicular—straight up and down.

groups, and the smallest group had ten lines. Unoka had a sense of the dramatic and so he allowed a pause, in which he took a pinch of <u>snuff</u> and sneezed noisily, and then he continued: "Each group there represents a debt to someone, and each stroke is one hundred cowries. You see, I owe that man a thousand cowries. But he has not come to wake me up in the morning for it. I shall pay you, but not today. Our elders say that the sun will shine on those who stand before it shines on those who kneel under them. I shall pay my big debts first." And he took another pinch of snuff, as if that was paying the big debts first. Okoye rolled his goatskin and departed.

?????????? STOP AND QUESTION ??????????

Is Unoka fair to Okoye? Explain.

....

....

....

....

When Unoka died he had taken no title at all and he was heavily in debt. Any wonder then that his son Okonkwo was ashamed of him? Fortunately, among these people a man was judged according to his worth and not according to the worth of his father. Okonkwo was clearly cut out for great things. He was still young but he had won fame as the greatest wrestler in the

VOCABULARY
snuff—tobacco.

"Okonkwo's Story" continued

nine villages. He was a wealthy farmer and had two barns full of <u>yams</u>, and had just married his third wife. To crown it all he had taken two titles and had shown incredible <u>prowess</u> in two <u>inter-tribal wars</u>. And so although Okonkwo was still young, he was already one of the greatest men of his time. Age was respected among his people, but achievement was <u>revered</u>. As the elders said, if a child washed his hands he could eat with kings. Okonkwo had clearly washed his hands and so he ate with kings and elders.

VOCABULARY
yams—edible plants.
prowess—skill.
inter-tribal wars—wars between tribes.
revered—greatly respected.

STOP AND SUMMARIZE STOP AND SUMMARIZE

What does the story suggest about parents and children?

....

....

....

....

....

....

....

Go back to page 59. Fill out the Anticipation/Reaction Guide, marking what really happened.

GATHER YOUR THOUGHTS

A. SUMMARIZE Think about both parts of the story. What does it say about Unoka as a father and Okonkwo as a son? Then answer these questions.

WHAT IS THIS STORY ABOUT?

WHAT **3** DETAILS FROM THE STORY SUPPORT THAT IDEA?

HOW WOULD YOU SUMMARIZE THE STORY?

B. USE A STORYBOARD On this storyboard, draw sketches of the action of the story. (Refer to your notes as needed.) Then write a 1-sentence explanation under each sketch.

C. CREATE A STORY PLOT Now create a plan to complete the story about an interesting character you started on page 57.
1. Review your story beginning.
2. Focus on the character's problem and how it will be worked out.
3. Then use the storyboard to show the action of your story.

1. At the beginning:

2. The problem:

3. What happens next:

4. Possible solution:

5. How it ends:

IV. WRITE

Write a draft of your **story** here.

1. Make sure your plot uses the character you wrote about in the last lesson.
2. Tell about the problem the character faces and how he or she solves it.
3. Use the Writers' Checklist to help you revise your draft.

Continue your writing on the next page.

WRITERS' CHECKLIST

DIALOGUE

☐ Did you use quotation marks around the direct words of a speaker? EXAMPLE: *"Why speak of it now?" she asked.*

☐ Did you use commas to set off a quotation from the rest of the sentence? EXAMPLE: *She looked at me and said, "Please don't touch a thing!"* If the quotation appears in the middle of the sentence, a comma is placed both before and after the quote. EXAMPLE: *Disgusted by my tone of voice, she muttered, "Leave me alone," and walked away.*

Continue your writing from the previous page.

WRAP-UP

V. What parts of Chinua Achebe's writing style did you like most or least?

Romance

Romance fuels the fire of love, keeping hearts warm and adding spark to people's lives. As long as love exists, the need for romance will never fade.

John Keats

Why would you want to read someone's letters? The letters can give a close-up glimpse into a person's life and how he or she thought. Consider this personal view of the English writer Barbara Pym. What can you learn from her letters and diary entries?

BEFORE YOU READ

Look at the photographs with the selection. What do the pictures tell you about the life and times in which Barbara Pym wrote?

1. Take a picture walk. Look through the pages of this lesson, thinking about the photos and their captions.
2. What do the photographs tell you about the life and times in which Barbara Pym wrote? Choose 3 photographs to write about below.

Picture Walk

The photo of . . .   tells me . . .

The photo of . . .   tells me . . .

The photo of . . .   tells me . . .

READ

Read through the letter and diary entries at your own pace.
1. As you read, **react** to what Pym says. ·······································
2. Connect her writings to events and people in your own life.

"Barbara Pym to Henry Harvey" by Barbara Pym

To Henry Harvey in Oxford

Staying with her cousin

Newburn,
Hatch End,
Middlesex.

15 May 1936

Dear Henry:

I don't know whether you intended me to answer your letter or whether it was just written in a hurry and you didn't mean a word you said. However it was quite sensible and much that you said I agreed with (look out!) but not all. If you want the truth straight away here it is. I am fed up with the whole business. Of writing gay flippant letters to you and expecting you to see that I didn't really feel that way. Of meeting you at regular intervals and finding that if anything we get on a little worse than the last time. Of having my peace disturbed for no purpose. And of your promises to write which never came to anything—although fair play to you—you always have plenty of excuses—and of finding that as time goes on you don't improve or grow any older—I mean grow up in the sense that people ought to.

EXAMPLE:
I've never written this kind of critical letter.

VOCABULARY
gay—cheerful.
flippant—casual; not serious.
intervals—periods of time.

Christ Church Cathedral in Oxford, England

React to Barbara Pym's writing. Choose words and phrases from her letter. Write them on the column on the left. On the right, write your reaction to the words and phrases.

Double-Entry Journal

Quotes	My Thoughts

Members of English society in the 1930s

EXAMPLE:

1. "Of meeting you at regular intervals and finding that if anything we get on a little worse than the last time."

This is a sign of a bad relationship.

2.

3.

Response Notes

"Barbara Pym to Henry Harvey" continued

In fact I <u>daresay</u> I've become thoroughly selfish and I feel like staying that way. Of course *all* this probably isn't your fault, although some of it certainly is. As you said, we have never been real to each other. This may be because of the way Jock has treated us by refusing to take anything seriously—but it is really because you haven't been <u>sufficiently</u> interested in me to make much effort about it. And of course when things are like that between two people there just isn't anything that can be done about it. I don't know whether you agree with me over this—or whether you've even thought about it, but I

VOCABULARY
daresay—feel almost certain; suppose.
sufficiently—enough.

"Barbara Pym to Henry Harvey" continued

think I am right. But however much Jock may be responsible for the state of affairs between us, I can never forget that he saved me a great deal of unhappiness by his way of looking at things, which I adopted too, at least in our <u>correspondence</u> and conversation. It is an amusing game, and I don't see why it should affect one's real self unless one wants it to. I know that as far as I'm concerned, although I've learned to treat things in his way, the other side of me is still there to be brought out when necessary. I have no wish that it should be <u>annihilated</u> altogether because I know I couldn't find any happiness unless I were a real person as well as a 'flat' one. (I use your word because it seems a good one and I can't think of another.

Choose a quote from Pym's letter. Write it in the column on the left. On the right, write your reaction to it.

Double-Entry Journal

Quote	My Thoughts

A photo of a couple in love, taken from the period in which Barbara Pym wrote.

VOCABULARY
correspondence—letters sent back and forth between two people.
annihilated—destroyed.

"Barbara Pym to Henry Harvey" continued

I'm finding it rather difficult to explain myself clearly, but I hope you'll see what I mean).

Did I tell you I had started a new novel? I am just beginning to get into form, although at first I found it something of an effort. It is about time my first novel came back from <u>Macmillan</u>—it has been there over two weeks now.

My best love to Mr. B. and Jock, and to you,

from Barbara

Write another quote from Pym's letter and then your thoughts about its meaning.

Double-Entry Journal

Quote	My Thoughts

"Diary Entry" by Barbara Pym

Oswestry. I've got to start writing again. I've fallen in love, and with Henry. I feel just as bad as I did three years ago—almost worse because he has been extremely nice to me and we have got on much better together than ever before. We have been together day and night for the past three weeks and yesterday he and Mr. B. brought me home and now I'm <u>wretched</u> and missing him terribly. I have been acting as his secretary since June 17th. I've typed and taken dictation and

VOCABULARY
Macmillan—book publishing company.
wretched—miserable.

"Diary Entry" continued

copied pages out of the *Dictionary of National Biography* for him—worked all night for him—and received 30/-a week.

    7 June. Oxford. On this day H., J., Mr. B., and I went out in the car for the day. Into the Cotswolds. But somehow I didn't get on very well with them. It was largely my own fault as I was inclined to be rather aggressive in my 'lowness,' talking about dance music etc. I think I did this because I felt intellectually inferior to them all, especially Henry, who always makes you feel it more than the others do. I felt that they were all against me and I made things worse by my obstinacy. But I felt resentful of being dominated by them and not being allowed to be myself at all. Also I was so conscious of being much better on paper than in speech. Anyway it was a nice day and we had a very pleasant dinner at the Old Swan at Minster Lovell, where we made up verses to celebrate the approaching nuptials of Count Weiss.

Read the quote in the left-hand column. Record your thoughts about it in the right-hand column.

Double-Entry Journal

Quote	My Thoughts
"Also I was so conscious of being much better on paper than in speech."	

VOCABULARY
'lowness'—inferiority.
obstinacy—stubbornness.
resentful—angry.
dominated—controlled.
conscious—aware.
nuptials—marriage.

Romantic couple from the 1940s in England

8 June. After tea Henry came round in the car to <u>fetch</u> me to hear a record of <u>James Joyce</u> at the flat. He was <u>morose</u> and bad tempered, hardly speaking to me and arguing with Jock I felt miserable and left rather <u>abruptly</u> before seven o'clock. Just as I was going Henry came to the door and said goodbye in that lovely gentle way of his which is so surprising. I often think that Henry is never so nice as when he's standing at the door of the flat saying goodbye.

9 June. I had a long talk with Mr. B. I can remember telling him that I thought I didn't care for Henry, in fact almost hated him at times, and wouldn't now marry him at any price, as I once thought I would.

Select another quote and write about it.

Double-Entry Journal

Quote	My Thoughts

VOCABULARY
fetch—take.
James Joyce—famous Irish writer (1882–1941).
morose—gloomy.
abruptly—suddenly.

GATHER YOUR THOUGHTS

A. PLAN Gather your thoughts as you plan a letter to a friend. Write about an experience that has happened to you in the last month.

1. To whom are you writing?

2. What experience will you write about in your letter?

B. RETELL AN EXPERIENCE Before you write your letter, think carefully about the experience you want to describe.

1. In the organizer below, write about the beginning, middle, and end of the experience.

2. End by stating your purpose for telling your friend about the experience.

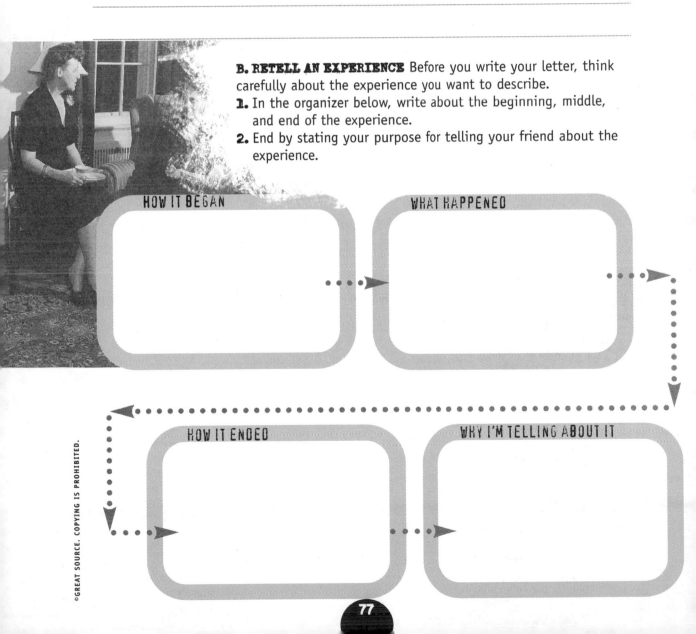

HOW IT BEGAN

WHAT HAPPENED

HOW IT ENDED

WHY I'M TELLING ABOUT IT

IV. WRITE

Now use your ideas to write a **letter** to a friend.

1. Look at the parts of a letter to use as a guide while you write.
2. Be sure to tell your friend about your experience and why you're writing about it.
3. Use the Writers' Checklist to help you revise.

Greeting
Dear and the name of the person to whom you are writing. The greeting ends with a comma.

Heading
Date you are writing the letter.

Body
The message of your letter.

WRITERS' CHECKLIST

CAPITALIZATION

☐ Did you capitalize names of people? (*Maria Torrez*)

☐ Did you capitalize titles of people used before proper names and in direct address? (*Dr. Bryan Terry*)

☐ In titles of books, movies, and songs, did you capitalize the first and last words and words other than articles and prepositions? (*Gone with the Wind*, "Home on the Range", *A Connecticut Yankee in King Arthur's Court*)

Closing
End with *Your friend,* or *Sincerely.* Capitalize the first word of the closing and end with a comma.

Signature
Sign your name.

V. WRAP-UP

What did you like or dislike about reading Barbara Pym's letter and diary?

Have you ever written any love letters? Have you ever received any? Even though love letters are not very common nowadays, people throughout the ages have told many of their deepest emotions in letters.

BEFORE YOU READ

Work with a partner. Take turns reading aloud the first part of the love letter on the next page.
1. Then complete the Listener's Guide below.
2. Discuss your answers with your partner.

Listener's Guide

What I already think about love and beauty:

_____

_____

_____

Words or phrases I noted:

_____ _____

_____ _____

_____ _____

_____ _____

(circle one)

I think this letter will be happy / sad.

(circle one)
I can / cannot relate to the experience of Keats and Franny Brawne in this letter.

II. READ

Read the letter, written in 1819, at your own pace.

1. As you read, circle any words or ideas that you don't understand.

2. Write any **questions** you have in the Response Notes.

"John Keats to Fanny Brawne" by John Keats

My sweet girl,—Your letter gave me more delight than anything in the world but yourself could do; indeed, I am almost astonished that any absent one should have that luxurious power over my senses which I feel. Even when I am not thinking of you, I perceive your tenderness and a tenderer nature stealing upon me. All my thoughts, my unhappiest days and nights, have I find not at all cured me of my love of Beauty, but made it so intense that I am miserable that you are not with me; or rather breathe in that dull sort of patience that cannot be called Life.

I never knew before, what such love as you have made me feel, was; I did not believe in it; my Fancy was afraid of it, lest it should burn me up. But if you will fully love me, though there may be some fire 'twill not be more than we can bear when moistened and bedewed with Pleasures.

EXAMPLE:
Why is he exaggerating his feelings so much?

Retell

Retell what you have read so far. How does Keats feel about Fanny Brawne?

_____

_____

_____

VOCABULARY
perceive—sense; see.
stealing—gracefully coming.
moistened—made wet.
bedewed—made wet with dew.

You mention "horrid people," and ask me whether it depends upon them whether I see you again. Do understand me, my love, in this. I have so much of you in my heart that I must turn Mentor, when I see a chance of harm befalling you. I would never see anything but Pleasure in your eyes, love on your lips, and Happiness in your steps. I would wish to see you among those amusements suitable to your inclinations and spirits so that our love might be a delight in the midst of Pleasures agreeable enough, rather than a resource from vexations and cares. But I doubt much, in case of the worst, whether I shall be philosopher enough to follow my own Lessons; if I saw my resolution give you a pain I could not. Why may I not speak of your Beauty, since without that I never could have lov'd you? I cannot conceive of any beginning of such love as I have for you but Beauty.

Retell

What is Keats telling Fanny about his love for her? Write what he is saying in your own words.

There may be a sort of love for which, without the least sneer at it, I have the highest respect and can admire it in others but it has not the richness, the bloom, the full form, the enchantment of love after my

VOCABULARY
horrid—dreadful.
Mentor—In Greek mythology, Mentor was Odysseus's trusted advisor and teacher. Here Keats means he will guard and protect Fanny.
befalling—happening to.
inclinations—tendencies; habits.
vexations—small things that annoy or bother.
conceive—think; understand.

"John Keats to Fanny Brawne" continued

own heart. So let me speak of your Beauty, though to my own endangering; if you could be so cruel to me as to try elsewhere its Power. You say I am afraid I shall think you do not love me—in saying this you make me ache the more to be near you.

I am at the <u>diligent</u> use of my <u>faculties</u> here, I do not pass a day without <u>scrawling</u> some blank verse or <u>tagging</u> some rhymes; and here I must confess that (since I am on the subject) I love you the more in that I believe you have liked me for my own sake and for nothing else. I have met with women whom I really think would like to be married to a Poem and to be given away by a Novel. I have seen your Comet, and only wish it was a sign that poor Rice would get well, whose illness makes him rather a <u>melancholy</u> companion. And the more so as to conquer his feelings and hide them from me, with a forc'd <u>Pun</u>. I kissed your writing over in the hope you had <u>indulged</u> me by leaving a trace of honey. What was your dream? Tell it to me and I will tell you the interpretation thereof.

Ever yours, my love!

John Keats.

Retell

What does Keats say he has been doing?

_____

_____

_____

_____

VOCABULARY
diligent—hard working.
faculties—abilities.
scrawling—scribbling.
tagging—writing the last lines of.
melancholy—gloomy.
Pun—play on words.
indulged—given into; gratified.

III GATHER YOUR THOUGHTS

A. FIND A SUBJECT What is there to write about? How do people think of things to write about?

1. Brainstorm a list of writing topics of your own.

2. Take a letter, such as **B**, and think of a several words that begin with that letter, as shown below.

3. Jot down 1 or 2 experiences that come to mind for each of those subjects.

Beautiful	Brave	Beliefs	Bad
_____	_____	_____	_____
_____	_____	_____	_____

B. DEVELOP YOUR SUBJECT Now choose the experience that you think is most interesting. Get ready to write about it in a journal entry.

1. Write the subject in the center of the graphic organizer below.

2. Develop the subject by answering the questions about it.

WHAT was the experience?

WHAT happened?

WHO was there?

HOW did you feel?

Subject: _____

WHY is this experience important?

WHEN and WHERE did the events take place?

IV. WRITE

Turn your ideas into a **journal entry**. Journal writing is personal, so you write about an experience or event that was important to you.

1. Begin with the date.
2. Then draft the entry, telling in detail about your subject.
3. Even though journal entries are informal, use the Writers' Checklist to help you revise.

WRITERS' CHECKLIST

CAPITALIZATION

❑ Did you capitalize the names of continents (*A*frica), countries (*J*apan), states (*R*hode *I*sland), counties (*O*range *C*ounty), and cities (*S*acramento)?

❑ Did you capitalize the names of specific bodies of water (*A*tlantic *O*cean), geographical names (*S*ahara *D*esert), regions (*C*entral *A*merica), and streets (*B*roadway *A*venue)?

❑ Did you capitalize the words *north*, *south*, *east*, and *west* when they refer to a specific area or are part of a proper name? Do not capitalize them when they tell direction. (the *F*ar *E*ast, the west coast of France, North Dakota, Drive south on *R*oute 57)

What made John Keats's letter easy or difficult to read?

READERS' CHECKLIST

EASE

☐ Was the selection easy to read?
☐ Were you able to read it smoothly and without difficulty?

Scientific Mysteries

Science has tried to answer many of life's mysteries. For example, how was the world formed? Why are some animals stronger and faster than others? As science answers some questions, it raises others.

Rachel Carson

Charles Darwin

Have you ever wondered how the earth was made? Ever imagine what life was like long ago? Scientists have written about the earth at the beginning of time. Try previewing science texts before you read. A preview can give you an idea of what the selection is about.

BEFORE YOU READ

Thumb through "The Gray Beginnings," part of Rachel Carson's book *The Sea Around Us*.

1. Pay attention to key words, photos, captions, and art.

2. Then make some notes on the Preview Guide.

PREVIEW GUIDE

Topic of the selection:

Subjects of photos and art:

Key words or phrases that caught my attention:

Idea from the first paragraph:

Idea from the last paragraph:

(circle one)

I think this article will be easy / difficult to read. Why?

READ

Read Rachel Carson's explanation about the beginning of the earth and its oceans.

1. Underline words, phrases, or ideas that you don't understand.

2. As you read, try to **clarify** what the author is saying by rewriting key points in your own words in the Response Notes.

"The Gray Beginnings" by Rachel Carson

RESPONSE NOTES

Beginnings are apt to be shadowy, and so it is with the beginnings of that great mother of life, the sea. Many people have <u>debated</u> how and when the earth got its ocean, and it is not surprising that their explanations do not always agree. For the plain and inescapable truth is that no one was there to see, and in the <u>absence</u> of eyewitness accounts there is bound to be a certain amount of disagreement. So if I tell here the story of how the young planet Earth <u>acquired</u> an ocean, it must be a story pieced together from many sources and containing whole chapters the details of which we can only imagine. The story is founded on the <u>testimony</u> of the earth's most ancient rocks, which were young when the earth was young; on other evidence written on the face of the earth's satellite, the moon; and on hints contained in the history of the sun and the whole universe of star-filled space. For although no man was there to witness this <u>cosmic</u> birth, the stars and moon and the rocks were there, and, indeed, had much to do with the fact that there is an ocean.

The events of which I write must have occurred somewhat more than 2 billion years ago. As nearly as science can tell, that is the <u>approximate</u> age of the earth, and the ocean must be very nearly as old.

EXAMPLE:
Rocks give clues about how the earth was made.

VOCABULARY
debated—argued.
absence—lack of.
acquired—got.
testimony—evidence.
cosmic—from another world; occurring outside of Earth.
approximate—almost exact.

stop and think

Where does Carson's story about the ocean come from?

....

....

What does Carson mean when she says, "Beginnings are apt to be shadowy . . ."?

....

....

....

RESPONSE NOTES

"The Gray Beginnings" CONTINUED

It is possible now to discover the age of the rocks that <u>compose</u> the crust of the earth by measuring the rate of decay of the <u>radioactive materials</u> they contain. The oldest rocks found anywhere on earth—in <u>Manitoba</u>— are about 2.3 billion years old. Allowing 100 million years or so for the cooling of the earth's materials to form a rocky crust, we arrive at the <u>supposition</u> that the <u>tempestuous</u> and violent events connected with our planet's birth occurred nearly 2½ billion years ago. But this is only a minimum estimate, for rocks indicating an even greater age may be found at any time.

The new earth, freshly torn from its parent sun, was a ball of whirling gases, intensely hot, rushing through the black spaces of the universe on a path and at a speed controlled by immense forces. Gradually the ball of flaming gases cooled. The gases began to <u>liquefy</u>, and Earth became a <u>molten</u> mass. The materials of this mass eventually became sorted out in a definite pattern: the

VOCABULARY
compose—make up; form.
radioactive materials—elements such as plutonium and radium.
Manitoba—province in Canada.
supposition—assumption.
tempestuous—turbulent; very strong.
liquefy—become liquid.
molten—melted.

"The Gray Beginnings" CONTINUED

heaviest in the center, the less heavy surrounding them, and the least heavy forming the outer rim. This is the pattern which persists today—a central sphere of molten iron, very nearly as hot as it was 2 billion years ago, an intermediate sphere of <u>semiplastic basalt</u>, and a hard outer shell, relatively quite thin and composed of solid basalt and <u>granite</u>.

stop and think

How did the earth change from a "ball of whirling gases" to the solid mass we know today?

_____

_____

_____

The outer shell of the young earth must have been a good many millions of years changing from the liquid to the solid state, and it is believed that, before this change was completed, an event of the greatest importance took place—the formation of the moon. The next time you stand on a beach at night, watching the moon's bright path across the water, and <u>conscious</u> of the moon-drawn tides, remember that the moon itself may have been born of a great tidal wave of earthly substance, torn off into space. And remember that if the moon was formed in this fashion, the event may have had much to do with shaping the <u>ocean basins</u> and the continents as we know them.

VOCABULARY

semiplastic basalt—hard, dark volcanic rock that's so hot it's soft and bendable.
granite—hard, coarse-grained rock.
conscious—aware.
ocean basins—bowl-shaped depressions on ocean floors.

A crater on the moon

"The Gray Beginnings" CONTINUED

There were tides in the new earth, long before there was an ocean. In response to the pull of the sun the molten liquids of the earth's whole surface rose in tides that rolled <u>unhindered</u> around the globe and only gradually <u>slackened</u> and <u>diminished</u> as the earthly shell cooled, <u>congealed</u>, and hardened. Those who believe that the moon is a child of Earth say that during an early stage of the earth's development something happened that caused this rolling, <u>viscid</u> tide to gather speed and momentum and to rise to unimaginable heights. Apparently the force that created these greatest tides the earth has ever known was the force of <u>resonance</u>, for at this time the period of the solar tides had come to approach, then equal, the period of the free <u>oscillation</u> of the liquid earth.

stop and think

According to Carson, how was the moon formed?

_____

_____

_____

_____

_____

The moon

VOCABULARY
unhindered—undisturbed; freely.
slackened—slowed down.
diminished—decreased.
congealed—changed from liquid to solid.
viscid—thick.
resonance—scientific term for increasing vibrations.
oscillation—moving back and forth.

"The Gray Beginnings" CONTINUED

And so every sun tide was given increased momentum by the push of the earth's oscillation, and each of the twice-daily tides was larger than the one before it. <u>Physicists</u> have calculated that, after 500 years of such monstrous, steadily increasing tides, those on the side toward the sun became too high for <u>stability</u>, and a great wave was torn away and hurled into space. But immediately, of course, the newly created satellite became subject to physical laws that sent it spinning in an <u>orbit</u> of its own about the earth. This is what we call the moon.

VOCABULARY
Physicists—scientists specializing in the study of matter and energy.
stability—steadiness.
orbit—path of something as it revolves around something else.

STOP AND REFLECT

What did you find most interesting about Carson's writing?

....

....

....

....

....

....

Now look back at the selection. With a partner, clarify the parts that were hard for you to understand.

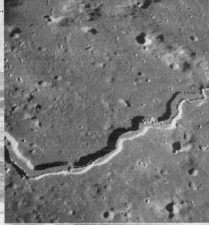

The surface of the moon

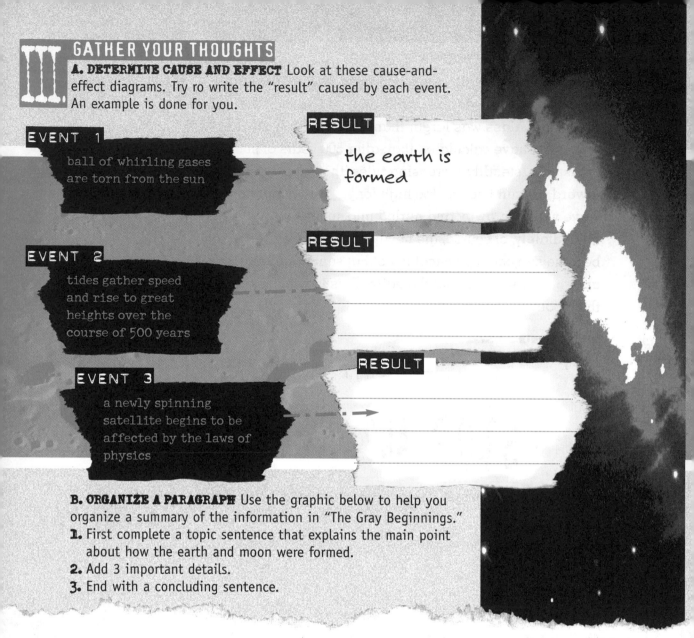

III GATHER YOUR THOUGHTS

A. DETERMINE CAUSE AND EFFECT Look at these cause-and-effect diagrams. Try ro write the "result" caused by each event. An example is done for you.

EVENT 1
ball of whirling gases are torn from the sun

RESULT
the earth is formed

EVENT 2
tides gather speed and rise to great heights over the course of 500 years

RESULT

EVENT 3
a newly spinning satellite begins to be affected by the laws of physics

RESULT

B. ORGANIZE A PARAGRAPH Use the graphic below to help you organize a summary of the information in "The Gray Beginnings."
1. First complete a topic sentence that explains the main point about how the earth and moon were formed.
2. Add 3 important details.
3. End with a concluding sentence.

TOPIC: _____

TOPIC SENTENCE

DETAIL	DETAIL	DETAIL

CONCLUDING SENTENCE

IV. WRITE

Write a **summary** about how the earth and moon were formed.
Explain it for students who are several years younger than you.
1. Begin with a topic sentence.
2. Add key details and end with a concluding sentence.
3. Use the Writers' Checklist to help you revise your summary.

Continue your writing on the next page.

Continue your writing from the previous page.

WRITERS' CHECKLIST

USAGE

❑ Did you use *bring* and *take* correctly? Use *bring* when the action is moving toward the speaker; use *take* when the action is moving away. EXAMPLES: *Please bring me that article. Then take that book out of here.*

❑ Did you use *learn* and *teach* correctly? *Learn* means "to get information," and *teach* means "to give information." EXAMPLE: *I will teach her to spell, but she'll have to learn to write on her own.*

V. WRAP-UP

How did you like "The Gray Beginnings"? Was it interesting? Why or why not?

READERS' CHECKLIST

ENJOYMENT

☐ Did you like the reading?

☐ Was the reading experience pleasurable?

☐ Would you want to reread the piece or recommend it to someone?

The earth as seen from outer space

10: The Struggle for Existence

You probably have heard the phrase "survival of the fittest," but what does it mean? It comes from the writing of Charles Darwin, an English scientist. Before reading about a topic, consider what you already know about it.

I. BEFORE YOU READ

The title of this selection is "The Struggle for Existence." Read the first sentence below.

> A struggle for existence <u>inevitably</u> follows from the high rate at which all <u>organic</u> beings tend to increase.

1. Think about what you already know about the subject of survival. Write your thoughts in the **K** column. Write questions you have in the **W** column.
2. After you've finished reading the piece, come back to complete the **L** column of the chart.

K-W-L CHART

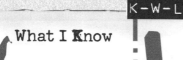

What I **K**now	What I **W**ant to Know	What I **L**earned

VOCABULARY
inevitably—invariably; unavoidably.
organic—natural.

READ

Now read this excerpt from Darwin's *The Origin of Species*.
1. Read slowly and carefully to yourself.
2. Then ask **questions** as you read, writing them in the Response Notes.

"The Struggle for Existence" by Charles Darwin

A struggle for existence inevitably follows from the high rate at which all organic beings tend to increase. Every being, which during its natural lifetime produces several eggs or seeds, must suffer destruction during some period of its life, and during some season or occasional year, otherwise, on the principle of geometrical increase, its numbers would quickly become so inordinately great that no country could support the product.

EXAMPLE:
Is Darwin talking about the problem of overpopulation?

One way to define an unfamiliar word or idea is to look for clues in the surrounding words and sentences. This is called "defining through the context." Any time you come across an unfamiliar word in your reading, first try to define it in context. If you get stuck, go to a dictionary.

WORD STUDY

KEY IDEAS	WHAT DOES IT MEAN?
the struggle for existence	EXAMPLE: It means "fight to live."
organic beings	

VOCABULARY
principle of geometric increase—mathematical sequence in which numbers increase in the same proportion, that is 2, 4, 8, 16, and so on.
inordinately—extremely.

RESPONSE NOTES

Hence, as more individuals are produced than can possibly survive, there must in every case be a struggle for existence, either one individual with another of the same species, or with the individuals of distinct species, or with the physical conditions of life. It is the <u>doctrine</u> <u>of</u> <u>Malthus</u> applied with <u>manifold</u> force to the whole animal and vegetable <u>kingdoms</u>; for in this case there can be no <u>artificial</u> increase of food, and no <u>prudential</u> <u>restraint</u> from marriage. Although some species may be now increasing, more or less rapidly, in numbers, all cannot do so, for the world would not hold them.

STOP aND THiNK

In your own words, what is Darwin saying in this paragraph?

_____

_____

_____

_____

_____

There is no exception to the rule that every organic being naturally increases at so high a rate, that if not destroyed, the earth would soon be covered by the <u>progeny</u> of a single pair.

Even slow-breeding man has doubled in twenty-five years, and at this rate, in a few thousand years, there

VOCABULARY

doctrine of Malthus—argument of a British economist, who in 1798 claimed that the population tended to increase faster than the food supply.
manifold—many kinds of; multiple.
kingdoms—divisions of classification. There are three main divisions—animal, vegetable, and mineral—into which objects are classified.
artificial—unnatural; man-made.
prudential—well judged; thought out.
restraint—limitation.
progeny—offspring.

"The Struggle for Existence" CONTINUED

would literally not be standing room for his progeny. Linnaeus has calculated that if an annual plant produced only two seeds—and there is no plant so unproductive as this—and their seedlings next year produced two, and so on, then in twenty years there would be a million plants. The elephant is reckoned to be the slowest breeder of all known animals, and I have taken some pains to estimate its probable minimum rate of natural increase: it will be under the mark to assume that it breeds when thirty years old, and goes on breeding till ninety years old, bringing forth three pairs of young in this interval; if this be so, at the end of the fifth century there would be alive fifteen million elephants, descended from the first pair.

But we have better evidence on this subject than mere theoretical calculations, namely, the numerous recorded cases of the astonishingly rapid increase of various animals in a state of nature, when circumstances have been favorable to them during two or three following seasons.

WORD STUDY

KEY IDEAS	WHAT DOES IT MEAN?
Linnaeus's theory of reproduction	
minimum rate of natural increase	

VOCABULARY
Linnaeus—Swedish botanist of the 1700s who came up with the modern classification system for plants and animals.
reckoned—considered.
state of nature—natural condition, unaffected by humans.

"The Struggle for Existence" CONTINUED

Still more striking is the evidence from our domestic animals of many kinds which have run wild in several parts of the world: if the statements of the rate of increase of slow-breeding cattle and horses in South America, and <u>latterly</u> in Australia, had not been well <u>authenticated</u>, they would have been quite incredible. So it is with plants: cases could be given of introduced plants which have become common throughout whole islands in a period of less than ten years. Several of the plants now most numerous over the wide plains of <u>La Plata</u>, <u>clothing</u> <u>square leagues of surface</u> almost to the exclusion of all other plants, have been introduced from Europe; and there are

plants which now range in India, as I hear from Dr. Falconer, from Cape Comorin to the <u>Himalaya</u>, which have been imported from America since its discovery.

VOCABULARY
latterly—later.
authenticated—proven; established as true.
La Plata—name for lands in South America controlled by the Spanish, which included Bolivia, Argentina, Uruguay, and Paraguay.
clothing—covering.
square leagues of surface—many square miles of land.
Himalaya—mountains in Asia.

"The Struggle for Existence" CONTINUED

In such cases, and endless instances could be given, no one supposes that the <u>fertility</u> of these animals or plants has been suddenly and temporarily increased in any sensible degree. The obvious explanation is that the conditions of life have been very favorable, and that there has consequently been less destruction of the old and young, and that nearly all the young have been enabled to breed. In such cases the geometrical ratio of increase, the result of which never fails to be surprising, simply explains the extraordinarily rapid increase and <u>wide diffusion of naturalized productions</u> in their new homes.

In a state of nature almost every plant produces seed, and amongst animals there are very few which do not annually pair. Hence we may confidently assert, that all plants and animals are tending to increase at a geometrical ratio, that all would most rapidly stock every station in which they could any how exist, and that the geometrical tendency to increase must be checked by destruction at some period of life. Our

VOCABULARY
fertility—birth rate.
wide diffusion of naturalized productions—widespread evidence of new life.

RESPONSE NOTES

familiarity with the larger <u>domestic animals</u> tends, I think, to mislead us: we see no great destruction falling on them, and we forget that thousands are annually slaughtered for food, and that in a state of nature an equal number would have somehow to be <u>disposed of</u>.

STOP AND THINK

What is Darwin's point about domestic animals?

....

....

....

....

The only difference between organisms which annually produce eggs or seeds by the thousand, and those which produce extremely few, is, that the slow-breeders would require a few more years to people, under favorable conditions, a whole district, let it be ever so large. The <u>condor</u> lays a couple of eggs and the <u>ostrich</u> a <u>score</u>, and yet in the same country the condor may be the more numerous of the two: the <u>Fulmar petrel</u> lays but one egg, yet it is believed to be the most numerous bird in the world. One fly deposits hundreds of eggs, and another, like the <u>hippobosca</u>, a single one; but this difference does not

VOCABULARY
domestic animals—tame animals such as pets.
disposed of—eliminated; gotten rid of.
condor—large bird common to South America.
ostrich—large bird common to Africa.
score—amount of twenty.
Fulmar petrel—smoky-gray bird common to the Arctic region.
hippobosca—kind of fly.

"The Struggle for Existence" CONTINUED

determine how many individuals of the two species can be supported in a district. A large number of eggs is of some importance to those species, which depend on a rapidly <u>fluctuating</u> amount of food, for it allows them rapidly to increase in number.

WORD STUDY

KEY IDEAS	WHAT DOES IT MEAN?
A fly depositing hundreds of eggs	

But the real importance of a large number of eggs or seeds is to make up for much destruction at some period of life; and this period in the great majority of cases is an early one. If an animal can in any way protect its own eggs or young, a small number may be produced, and yet the average stock be fully kept up; but if many eggs or young are destroyed, many must be produced, or the species will become <u>extinct</u>. It would suffice to keep up the full number of a tree, which lived on an average for a thousand years, if a single seed were produced once in a thousand years, supposing that this seed were never destroyed, and could be ensured to <u>germinate</u> in a fitting place. So that in all cases, the average number of any animal or plant depends only indirectly on the number of its eggs or seeds.

In looking at Nature, it is most necessary to keep the foregoing considerations always in mind—never to forget that every single organic being around us may be said to be striving to the <u>utmost</u> to increase in numbers; that each lives by a struggle at some period of its life; that heavy destruction inevitably falls either on the

VOCABULARY
fluctuating—changing.
extinct—no longer alive.
germinate—grow.
utmost—highest degree.

RESPONSE NOTES

young or old, during each generation or at <u>recurrent</u> intervals. Lighten any check, <u>mitigate</u> the destruction ever so little, and the number of the species will almost <u>instantaneously</u> increase to any amount. The face of Nature may be compared to a yielding surface, with ten thousand sharp wedges packed close together and driven inwards by <u>incessant</u> blows, sometimes one wedge being struck, and then another with greater force.

What checks the natural tendency of each species to increase in number is most <u>obscure</u>. Look at the most vigorous species; by as much as it swarms in numbers, by so much will its tendency to increase be still further increased. We know not exactly what the checks are in even one single instance. Nor will this surprise any one who reflects how ignorant we are on this head, even in regard to mankind, so incomparably better known than any other animal.

STOP AND THINK

What is the main idea of Darwin's article?

....

....

....

....

VOCABULARY
recurrent—happening again and again.
mitigate—lessen;
instantaneously—instantly; immediately.
incessant—continuing.
obscure—unclear.

GATHER YOUR THOUGHTS

A. SUPPORT THE THESIS In a well-written essay, the author gives plenty of support for the thesis, or main idea. Darwin looks to the natural world to support his ideas.

1. Look back at his essay. Find 3 examples, short stories, or facts that support his idea that *the struggle for existence must occur*.
2. Write the supporting details here.

SUPPORTING DETAIL 1	SUPPORTING DETAIL 2	SUPPORTING DETAIL 3

B. WRITE A THESIS Think about some of the ideas raised by Darwin's essay:

survival of the fittest

controlling overpopulation

variety of plants and animals

1. Plan to write a 3-paragraph essay about 1 of these topics. Circle your choice.
2. Draft a thesis statement about your topic, following the model below.
3. Write your thesis statement on the lines below.

Thesis statement: The importance of

is . . .

C. PLAN AN ESSAY Think through a 3-paragraph essay you will write about the topic you chose. Plan what you will say in each paragraph by answering the questions below.

INTRODUCTION

What is the idea?

SUPPORT

What examples or evidence support the idea?

CONCLUSION

Why is the idea important?

IV. WRITE

Write a **3-paragraph essay** about the idea you chose from "The Struggle for Existence."

1. Use your notes from the previous page as a guide to write your essay.

2. Use the Writers' Checklist to help you revise.

Continue your writing on the next page.

WRITERS' CHECKLIST

MISPLACED MODIFIERS

❏ **Did you check for misplaced modifiers? Misplaced modifiers are descriptive words that have been placed incorrectly. They make your writing confusing and unclear. Keep modifiers placed as closely as possible to the words they modify.** EXAMPLES: *Incorrect: In the mouse hole, the child watched the mouse. (The child is in the mouse hole?) correct: The child watched the mouse in the mouse hole.*

Continue your writing from the previous page.

V. WRAP-UP

In your own words, what was the main idea of "The Struggle for Existence"?

Virginia Woolf

Born in England, Virginia Woolf (1882–1941) wrote many novels and essays. Woolf is noted for her feminist values, keen observation, and thoughtful writing style.

How good are you as an observer? How well do you notice what goes on around you? Writers tend to be excellent observers of the world around them. Small things—such as the death of an insect—carry a lot of meaning for an observant writer.

BEFORE YOU READ

Read through the questions below. Then go on a fact-finding mission in the selection.

1. Walk through the selection with these questions in mind. Spend just 1–2 minutes skimming through it.

2. Then answer the questions.

Walk-through

1. What seems to be the subject?

2. What's the setting?

3. Who is it about?

4. What do you think will happen?

5. What do the pictures suggest this essay is about?

II. READ

Read the essay at your own pace.

1. As you read, revisit the questions you considered during the walk-through of the selection.

2. **Mark** or **highlight** any information that helps answer those questions. Jot down your ideas in the Response Notes.

Response Notes

"The Death of the Moth" by Virginia Woolf

Moths that fly by day are not properly to be called moths; they do not excite that pleasant sense of dark autumn nights and ivy-blossom which the commonest yellow underwing asleep in the shadow of the curtain never fails to rouse in us. They are hybrid creatures, neither gay like butterflies nor somber like their own species.

Nevertheless the present specimen, with his narrow hay colored wings, fringed with a tassel of the same seemed to be content with life. It was a pleasant morning, mid-September, mild, benignant, yet with a keener breath than that of the summer months. The plough was already scoring the field opposite the window, and where the share had been, the earth was pressed flat and gleamed with moisture. Such vigor came rolling in from the fields and the down beyond that it was difficult to keep the eyes strictly turned upon the book. The rooks too were keeping one of their annual festivities; soaring round the tree tops until it looked as if a vast net with thousands of black knots in it had been cast up into the air; which, after a few moments sank slowly down upon the trees until every

EXAMPLE:
setting = a fall
day in the country

VOCABULARY
hybrid—of mixed origin.
somber—dark; gloomy.
specimen—individual.
tassel—bunch of loose threads.
benignant—favorable.
keener—sharper; stronger.
scoring—marking.
rooks—birds similar to crows.
annual—yearly.

twig seemed to have a knot at the end of it. Then, suddenly, the net would be thrown into the air again in a wider circle this time, with the utmost clamor and vociferation, as though to be thrown into the air and settle slowly down upon the tree tops were a tremendously exciting experience.

stop+think

What is the mood or feeling of the essay so far?

....

....

stop+think

The same energy which inspired the rooks, the ploughmen, the horses, and even, it seemed, the lean bare-backed downs, sent the moth fluttering from side to side of his square of the windowpane. One could not help watching him. One was, indeed, conscious of a queer feeling of pity for him. The possibilities of pleasure seemed that morning so enormous and so various that to have only a moth's part in life, and a day moth's at that, appeared a hard fate, and his zest in enjoying his meager opportunities to the full, pathetic. He flew vigorously to one corner of his compartment, and, after waiting there a second, flew across to the other. What remained for him but to fly to a third corner and then to a fourth? That was all he could do, in spite of the size of the downs, the width of the sky, the far-off smoke of houses, and the romantic voice, now and then, of a steamer out at sea. What he could do he did.

VOCABULARY
vociferation—noise.
zest—interest.
meager—few; scanty.
pathetic—pitiful; sad.
steamer—kind of ship.

"The Death of the Moth" continued

Watching him, it seemed as if a fiber, very thin but pure, of the enormous energy of the world had been thrust into his frail and <u>diminutive</u> body. As often as he crossed the pane, I could fancy that a thread of <u>vital</u> light became visible. He was little or nothing but life.

stop + think

How does the narrator feel about the moth?

stop + think

Yet, because he was so small, and so simple a form of the energy that was rolling in at the open window and driving its way through so many narrow and <u>intricate</u> <u>corridors</u> in my own brain and in those of other human beings, there was something marvelous as well as pathetic about him. It was as if someone had taken a tiny bead of pure life and decking it as lightly as possible with down and feathers, had set it dancing and zigzagging to show us the true nature of life. Thus displayed one could not get over the strangeness of it. One is apt to forget all about life, seeing it <u>humped</u> and <u>bossed</u> and <u>garnished</u> and <u>cumbered</u> so that it has to move with the greatest <u>circumspection</u> and dignity. Again, the thought of all that life might have been had he been born in any other shape caused one to view his simple activities with a kind of pity.

VOCABULARY
diminutive—extremely small.
vital—essential; energetic.
intricate—elaborate.
corridors—hallways.
humped—arched.
bossed—raised.
garnished—decorated.
cumbered—weighed down.
circumspection—caution.

GATHER YOUR THOUGHTS

A. GATHER DESCRIPTIVE WORDS Go back through the selection and look for words or phrases the author uses to describe the moth. List them in the boxes below.

LOOKS	FEELINGS	ACTIONS

B. CREATE A DESCRIPTION To make your writing descriptive, you need to use your powers of observation.

1. Find an animal, insect, or object. Look at it very carefully for about 60 seconds.

2. Then get ready to write a descriptive paragraph by answering the questions below.

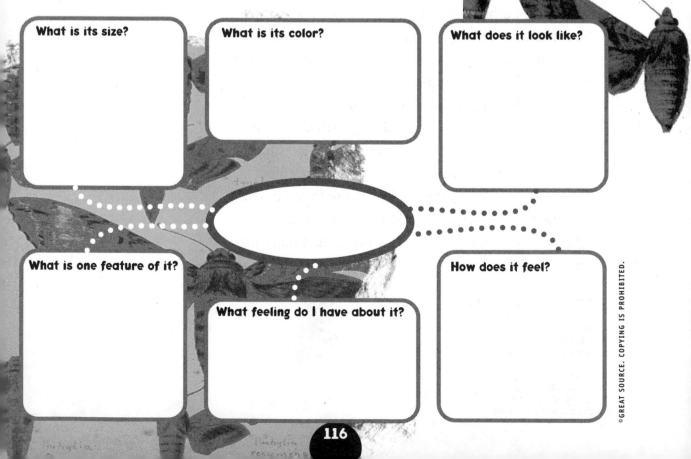

What is its size?

What is its color?

What does it look like?

What is one feature of it?

What feeling do I have about it?

How does it feel?

IV. WRITE

Write a **descriptive paragraph** about the subject you chose.

1. Before you begin writing, number the details in your organizer in the order you want to present them.
2. Then draft your paragraph, using descriptive words and phrases to paint a picture of your subject.
3. Use the Writers' Checklist to help you revise the paragraph.

WRITERS' CHECKLIST

USAGE

☐ Did you use *good, better,* and *best* correctly? *Better* is the comparative form of *good.* Use the word when you are comparing two things. EXAMPLE: *A day in the fall is better than a day in the spring. Best* is the superlative form of *good.* Use *best* when you are comparing more than two things. EXAMPLE: *Summer days are best of all.*

☐ Did you remember to avoid double comparisons that use both –er or –est and *more* or *most?* EXAMPLES: *The moth flew in a more wider circle.(incorrect) The moth flew in a wider circle. (correct)*

V. WRAP-UP

What do you find most interesting about the way that Virginia Woolf writes?

Are you a person who tries to guess how movies end? Then you probably know you can do the same thing when reading. Take a moment to think ahead and ask yourself, "How is this going to end?"

I. BEFORE YOU READ

One easy way of looking ahead is to use an Anticipation Guide. It asks questions about what you think will happen.

1. Answer each of the questions below.
2. Then compare your answers with a partner. Discuss where you agreed and where you disagreed.
3. End by making a prediction about how "The Death of the Moth" will end.

Anticipation Guide

AGREE   DISAGREE

1. **Virginia Woolf is trying to show what extraordinary insects moths are.**

2. **The most important word in her title is probably "death," not "moth."**

3. **The author saves the moth from death by rescuing it from a hungry spider.**

4. **Woolf admires the moth's struggle for life, even though no one seemingly cares if the moth lives or dies.**

I predict the ending of the essay will be . . .

_____

_____

_____

_____

_____

II. READ

Now read the rest of Virginia Woolf's essay "The Death of the Moth."

1. Think about why Woolf is interested in the moth.

2. Jot down any **questions** you have or would like to ask the author in the Response Notes.

Response Notes

EXAMPLE:

Did Woolf think it was strange to keep paying attention to the moth?

"The Death of the Moth" (continued) by Virginia Woolf

After a time, tired by his dancing apparently, he settled on the window ledge in the sun, and, the queer spectacle being at an end, I forgot about him. Then, looking up, my eye was caught by him. He was trying to <u>resume</u> his dancing, but seemed either so stiff or so awkward that he could only flutter to the bottom of the window-pane; and when he tried to fly across it he failed. Being intent on other matters I watched these <u>futile</u> attempts for a time without thinking, <u>unconsciously</u> waiting for him to resume his flight, as one waits for a machine, that has stopped momentarily, to start again without considering the reason of its failure. After perhaps a seventh attempt he slipped from the wooden ledge and fell, fluttering his wings, on to his back on the window sill. The helplessness of his attitude roused me. It flashed upon me that he was in difficulties; he could no longer raise himself; his legs struggled <u>vainly</u>. But, as I stretched out a pencil, meaning to help him to right himself, it came over me that the failure and awkwardness were the approach of death. I laid the pencil down again.

stop+clarify

What do these events tell the author about the moth?

stop+clarify

VOCABULARY

resume—begin again.
futile—useless.
unconsciously—without knowing or realizing.
vainly—without success.

"The Death of the Moth" continued

The legs agitated themselves once more. I looked as if for the enemy against which he struggled. I looked out of doors. What had happened there? Presumably it was midday, and work in the fields had stopped. Stillness and quiet had replaced the previous animation. The birds had taken themselves off to feed in the brooks. The horses stood still. Yet the power was there all the same, massed outside indifferent, impersonal, not attending to anything in particular. Somehow it was opposed to the little hay-colored moth. It was useless to try to do anything. One could only watch the extraordinary efforts made by those tiny legs against an oncoming doom which could, had it chosen, have <u>submerged</u> an entire city, not merely a city, but masses of human beings; nothing, I knew, had any chance against death.

stop+predict

What will happen to the moth next?

_____

_____

_____

stop+predict

Nevertheless after a pause of exhaustion the legs fluttered again. It was superb this last protest, and so <u>frantic</u> that he succeeded at last in righting himself. One's sympathies, of course, were all on the side of life. Also, when there was nobody to care or to know, this gigantic effort on the part of an insignificant little moth, against a power of such <u>magnitude</u>, to retain what no one else valued or desired to keep, moved one

VOCABULARY
submerged—flooded; covered.
frantic—frustrated; highly excited.
magnitude—greatness; large size.

strangely. Again, somehow, one saw life, a pure bead. I lifted the pencil again, useless though I knew it to be.

stop+question

What questions does this essay raise for you?

stop+question

But even as I did so, the unmistakable <u>tokens</u> of death showed themselves. The body relaxed, and instantly grew stiff. The struggle was over. The insignificant little creature now knew death. As I looked at the dead moth this <u>minute</u> <u>wayside</u> triumph of so great a force over so mean an <u>antagonist</u> filled me with wonder. Just as life had been strange a few minutes before, so death was now as strange. The moth having righted himself now lay most decently and uncomplainingly <u>composed</u>. O yes, he seemed to say, death is stronger than I am.

VOCABULARY
tokens—proofs.
minute—tiny.
wayside—the side or edge of a path. In this case, *wayside* means insignificant.
antagonist—opponent; competitor.
composed—calm.

Summarize

How would you summarize "The Death of the Moth" in a few sentences?

GATHER YOUR THOUGHTS

A. BRAINSTORM TOPICS Virginia Woolf took an everyday event and looked at the deeper significance of it. List 3–5 ordinary events from your own life that you might like to write about.

POSSIBLE TOPICS

1.
2.
3.
4.
5.

B. EXPLORE A SUBJECT Think about 1 event you listed and reflect on its larger meaning. Then write what you think might be its deeper significance.

EXAMPLE:

moth runs into a windowpane

| Like the moth, we all struggle to survive. | Like the moth, we all die quietly and alone. |

Event

Significance:

Significance:

B. DEVELOP A SUBJECT Use the everyday event you chose to be the subject of a reflective paragraph.

1. Complete the storyboard below to tell the story of the event.

2. End with a reflection on what the event suggests to you.

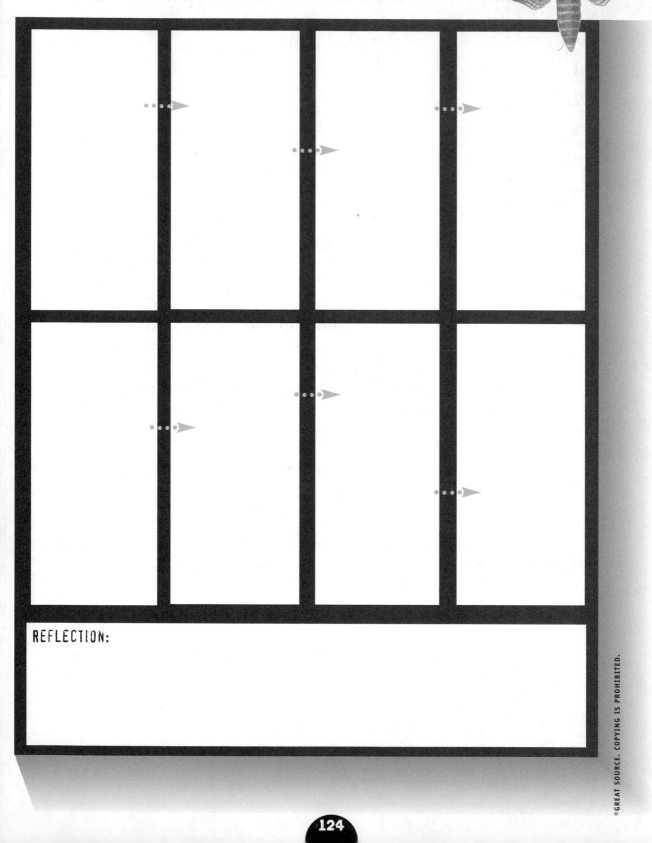

REFLECTION:

IV. WRITE

Now write a **reflective paragraph** about the everyday event.
1. Use the storyboard on the previous page to tell the important details of what happened.
2. End with a reflective sentence or two that tell what you think the significance of the event was.
3. Use the Writers' Checklist to help you revise.

WRITERS' CHECKLIST

COMMAS

☐ Did you use a comma in dates? EXAMPLE: My birthday is October 12, 1985.

☐ Did you use a comma to set off words or names used in direct address? EXAMPLE: Miranda, did you notice the moth?

☐ Did you use a comma after an interjection, such as okay or well or after an introductory word such as yes or no? EXAMPLES: Yes, I saw it this morning. Okay, I agree with you.

V. WRAP-UP

What did Virginia Woolf's essay make you think about?

READERS' CHECKLIST

DEPTH

❑ Did the reading make you think about things?
❑ Did it set off thoughts beyond the surface topic?

_____

_____

_____

_____

_____

_____

_____

_____

_____

_____

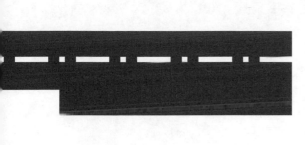

Violence

Is violence a part of human nature? Or is it something people learn as a result of their surroundings? Is violence ever necessary? Or is it used merely because it offers an easy solution?

What things do you know about? You probably know a lot more than you think you do. Most of us just need a way to connect with what we are reading to unleash all that we know. Then, with one simple connection, the reading becomes easier and clearer.

I. BEFORE YOU READ

Read the 3 questions below.
1. Decide which question you can connect to the most easily or which one interests you the most.
2. Quickwrite an answer to the question. Write for 1 minute.
3. Then share what you wrote with the rest of the class.

QUESTION #1
What is the worst accident you ever witnessed?

QUESTION #2
What can you do or say to comfort someone who is grieving?

QUESTION #3
Is it really true that your entire life can change in just one minute?

1-MINUTE QUICKWRITE

QUESTION # ___

READ

Now read Peter Kumalo's story "Death in the Sun."
1. As you read, pay attention to how Kumalo begins and ends his story.
2. **Visualize** the events in the story by making sketches of key scenes.

"Death in the Sun" by Peter Kumalo

That day coming into Cape Town by bus with two friends, I saw the stark tragedy of the drama of Life and Sudden Death played out in reality below the <u>precincts</u> of District Six and with this new experience I felt naked and afraid.

Slowly moving off from a stop our bus approached Tennant Street and a man came dashing around that corner into the main road hotly pursued by a young fellow leading a gang of youths who followed some paces behind.

STOP AND PREDICT

What do you think will happen to the man being chased?

....

....

....

STOP AND PREDICT

They ran on for about thirty yards and the gang leader had almost caught hold of the fleeing man when he with amazing swiftness halted in his tracks, turned and struck at him and it was only after the action had been completed, when he lifted his hand, that we, watching in the bus, saw the knife and the shocking realization came to us that he had stabbed the young fellow. He then turned again and fled on and the stabbed fellow stopped, looked at his chest and it was as if he too suddenly realized what had happened to

RESPONSE NOTES

EXAMPLE:

VOCABULARY
precincts—police stations.

him in that split second and when he turned there was a growing red stain on his shirt and we could see the surprise on his face, shock, fright, the desire to go on living, not to die in the instant he faced our way. He shouted, "O God, help me!" and started running toward the rear of our bus while the blood ran streaming out from between the fingers of his left hand which he held to his heart as if to stem the flow—all the while the bus moving very slowly with only a murmur coming from its engine and the passengers petrified into attitudes of astonishment, unable to utter words.

STOP AND PREDICT

What do you think the people on the bus will do?

....

....

....

....

STOP AND PREDICT

Then we tried to get down from the upper deck where we had been sitting to the lower deck, but a passenger stopped on his way halfway down the stairs, halted by momentary shock at what he saw and we could get no farther until we had pushed him aside and forced our way through.

There was a patch of blood from the dying-man's hand on the shiny chrome-steel bar which he had clutched in an effort to pull himself onto the platform and he was now lying in the aisle on his back with his legs bent under him and his arms thrown back like a person who had been struck down while kneeling at prayer. His shirt was soaked red and his trousers and the seats and the floor were splashed with blood.

VOCABULARY
petrified—stiffened.
chrome-steel—hard, metallic.

RESPONSE NOTES

His chest heaved a great effort as he breathed, his shirt drawing tight every few seconds along the edge of his rib-cage as he inhaled. In his open eyes, unstaring and looking at no one in particular, one could see emotional conflict and horror at the crazy and frightening knowledge that that amazing thing, Death, was so very near and that he was so very alone and that all the while his life's blood was steadily pouring out of his pierced heart. And, we, we felt so helpless, so terribly helpless because we could do nothing to save his young, tender life.

And death, when it came, was sudden—like the disappearance of the golden setting sun when one's back is turned, like the unexpected <u>toll</u> of a bell in the still of night and his body was that of a person from whom the personality had been erased, a corpse as lifeless as a dead limp impersonal doll from which human blood <u>frothed</u> and left a <u>crimson</u> trail as it flowed on the floor and over the hard steel edge of the platform onto the hot surface of the <u>asphalt</u> road.

STOP AND PREDICT

What do you think will happen now?

....

....

....

....

There was some panic among the passengers but some people, when the bus stopped, ran to get help, to telephone for the doctor, for the ambulance, for the police and a <u>gaping</u>, <u>milling</u> crowd gathered, people

VOCABULARY
toll—ring.
frothed—foamed.
crimson—dark red.
asphalt—paved.
gaping—staring.
milling—confused; disorderly.

RESPONSE NOTES

out of the slums from which this young man had come to meet death, <u>tawdry</u>, <u>workworn</u>, some dressed in soiled clothing, housewives with <u>unkempt</u> hair and dirty aprons, a few drunken men, barefoot children whose attention had suddenly been arrested from play, all excited, all curious and wanting to have a look and when they saw were hushed into an uncomfortable, questioning silence at this hostile, unwanted presence cast suddenly into their midst. And all the time there was a hum of conversation that was a <u>quavering drone</u> of excited voices above which rose certain questions and explanations, "Loep haal sy ma," said one woman's voice.

And others said, "Wat is sy naam?" and "Dis daai klong wat hier bo in Tennantstraat bly" . . . "Wattit gabeur" . . . "Haai, kyk die bloed!" But above all, "Is hy dood?"

And very few people certain enough dared to answer that he was dead because even they <u>unconsciously</u> were hoping that he was still alive, that he must still be alive so they hardly answered but kept silent unwilling tongues.

And then the gasping crowd's movement increased as more people tried to force a way through to the front and somebody said, "Vooitog, dis sy pa and ma."

STOP AND PREDICT

What will happen next?

....

....

....

....

VOCABULARY
tawdry—cheap-looking.
workworn—worn out; tired-looking.
unkempt—untidy; messy.
quavering drone—shaky murmuring sound.
unconsciously—without realizing; unknowingly.

"Death in the Sun" continued

And there were over-anxious, frightened, pitying looks on the faces of the people. A weeping child fought his way through the swaying mass and somebody else said, "Shame, that's his small brother," and he went into the bus to his dead brother, wanting

him alive and finding him dead, almost maddened by his great grief, ran toward an approaching car in an attempt to destroy himself under its wheels but was pulled back. People struggled to move aside so as to make way for the dead youth's parents to come through who were sobbing and crying and who, when they saw their son, fell into <u>paroxysms of hysteria</u> and the mother in her agony tore at her hair like a <u>demented</u> being and friends of theirs tried to comfort them and to lead them away, but they would not go and leave the body alone.

The ambulance and the police arrived <u>simultaneously</u> with a siren blaring a way through and there were men in uniforms with authority in their voices, organizing and bringing order among the throng and asking questions and the body was picked up and taken away and then the police sped off to catch up with the mob who had gone to hunt for the murderer and which by now had long since disappeared down a side street by the market place in the distance. And when authority had gone and the cause of it all, the crowd broke up, gradually and unwillingly, still asking questions and latecomers

VOCABULARY

paroxysms of hysteria—outbursts of great emotion.
demented—crazy.
simultaneously—at the same time.

RESPONSE NOTES

listened hungrily to <u>vague</u> explanations from those who still stood about.

And the afternoon sun shone, a great glowing ball suspended in the afternoon sky, fierce in its summer heat, casting its warm <u>radiant</u> light like a golden mantle, but for a little group of three people its light had gone out suddenly as if a great black cloud had descended and they were left weeping in <u>unbounded</u> darkness.

VOCABULARY
vague—unclear.
radiant—glowing.
unbounded—endless.

STOP AND SUMMARIZE STOP AND SUMMARIZE

What are the 5 main events in this story?

1.

2.

3.

4.

5.

GATHER YOUR THOUGHTS

A. DEVELOP A STORY Think of a dramatic event you saw and would like to write a paragraph about.

1. Write details of the beginning, middle, and end of the event in the boxes.

2. Reflect on what the story means in the "What It Means" box.

BEGINNING

MIDDLE

END

WHAT IT MEANS

B. PLAN A NARRATIVE Now plan to write a narrative paragraph of your own.

1. Review the details you listed on the previous page.

2. Then make notes about it on the Planning Chart below.

PLANNING CHART

PLANNING QUESTIONS	MY NOTES
Where did the incident or event take place?	
When did it occur?	
What happened?	
Why did it happen?	
Who was involved?	
How did the experience make you feel?	

C. BEGIN A STORY Stories begin a number of different ways, but often they begin just before the most important event. "Death in the Sun," for example, began right before the fight in the street.

1. Write the most important action of your story in the bottom box.

2. Then write what happens just before that moment in the top box. Use that as the beginning of your narrative paragraph.

	A MOMENT BEFORE

MOST IMPORTANT ACTION	

IV. WRITE

Now write a **narrative paragraph** about a dramatic event you saw.
1. Begin your paragraph right before the main action occurs.
2. Include details that will help make clear the significance of the event.
3. Use the Writers' Checklist to help you revise.

WRITERS' CHECKLIST

COMMAS

☐ Did you use a comma between coordinate adjectives not joined by *and*? EXAMPLE: *The sad, scared boy buried his face in his coat.*

☐ Did you use a comma to set off transitional words and parenthetical expressions? EXAMPLE: *Finally, I managed to calm down and take a deep breath.*

What point did you take away from Kumalo's "Death in the Sun"?

14: Charge of the Light Brigade

Alfred, Lord Tennyson

Are you one of those people who finds poems hard to read? Do you worry you are not getting it? If so, try something different. Try to find a personal connection to the poem. Look for a link—any tie—between yourself and the poem. Part of understanding poetry is understanding what it means <u>to you</u>.

BEFORE YOU READ

Get together with a reading partner.

1. Listen as your partner reads aloud the first part of the poem on the next page.

2. Then work with your partner to answer these questions.

1. Who is the poem about?

2. Where does the action take place?

3. What happens?

4. What do you think the title means?

5. What personal connection can you make to the poem?

READ ALOUD

Take turns with your partner reading "The Charge of the Light Brigade" aloud.

1. As you read, **clarify** any lines you are not sure of in the Response Notes.

2. Think about how you can relate the poem to your own life.

RESPONSE NOTES

EXAMPLE:
Many soldiers died there.

"The Charge of the Light Brigade"
by Alfred, Lord Tennyson

Half a <u>league</u>, half a league,
Half a league onward,
All in the valley of Death
   Rode the six hundred.
"Forward the Light Brigade!
Charge for the guns!" he said.
Into the valley of Death
Rode the six hundred.

"Forward, the Light Brigade!"
Was there a man dismayed?
Not though the soldier knew
   Someone had <u>blundered</u>.
Theirs not to make reply,
Theirs not to reason why,
Theirs but to do and die.
Into the valley of Death
   Rode the six hundred.

VOCABULARY

league—unit of distance equal to about three miles.
blundered—made a mistake.

140

Jot down some of your own thoughts about Tennyson's lines.
1. In the left column write words and lines from the poem that are interesting or that you like the sound of.
2. In the right column, respond to the quotes.

QUOTES	MY THOUGHTS
EXAMPLE: "Theirs not to make reply, / Theirs not to reason why. . . ."	This probably means that the men weren't allowed to object or disagree. They had to go into battle.

"The Charge of the Light Brigade" continued

Cannon to right of them,
Cannon to left of them,
Cannon in front of them
    Volleyed and thundered;
Stormed at with shot and shell,
Boldly they rode and well,
Into the jaws of Death,
Into the mouth of hell
    Rode the six hundred.

Flashed all their sabers bare,
Flashed as they turned in air
Sab'ring the gunners there,
Charging an army, while
    All the world wondered.
Plunged in the battery smoke
Right through the line they broke;

VOCABULARY
Volleyed—shot at.
sabers—heavy swords.
battery—artillery.

RESPONSE NOTES

<u>Cossack</u> and Russian
<u>Reeled</u> from the saber stroke
　　Shattered and <u>sundered</u>.
Then they rode back, but not,
　　Not the six hundred.
Cannon to right of them,
Cannon to left of them,
Cannon behind them
　　Volleyed and thundered;
Stormed at with shot and shell,
While horse and hero fell.
They that had fought so well
Came through the jaws of Death,
Back from the mouth of hell,
All that was left of them,
　　Left of six hundred.

When can their glory fade?
O the wild charge they made!
　　All the world wondered.
Honor the charge they made!
Honor the Light Brigade,
　　Noble six hundred!

VOCABULARY
Cossack—South Russian.
Reeled—thrown off balance.
sundered—separated.

DOUBLE-ENTRY JOURNAL

Select a quote that interests you and write your thoughts about it.

QUOTE	MY THOUGHTS

GATHER YOUR THOUGHTS

A. REFLECT Think about the poem you just read. Then answer these questions.

What was the Charge of the Light Brigade?

What are some of the lines that are repeated?

How can you connect the poem to your life?

B. BRAINSTORM Choose 1 of the words below as the subject of a poem of your own.
1. Circle the idea that seems to you the closest to "The Charge of the Light Brigade."
2. Then brainstorm other words suggested by that idea. An example for *fighting* is done for you.

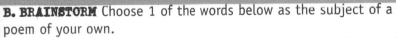

FIGHTING   HEROISM   BRAVERY

SIGHTS	SOUNDS	PEOPLE	FEELINGS
			EXAMPLE: fear

C. PLAN A POEM Complete the following sentences as a way of planning your poem.

My poem will be about . . .

I want my poem to . . .

The title of my poem will be . . .

D. USE A MODEL Use the first stanza (8 lines) of "The Charge of the Light Brigade" as a general model for your poem.

1. Make your poem 8 lines long.

2. Repeat the same phrase in the first and second lines of your poem, just as Tennyson repeats the phrase "Half a league."

3. Use the space below to draft ideas for your poem's opening couple of lines.

MODEL:

Half a <u>league</u>, half a league,
Half a league onward,
All in the valley of Death
   Rode the six hundred.
"Forward the Light Brigade!
Charge for the guns!" he said.
Into the valley of Death
Rode the six hundred.

IDEAS FOR OPENING LINES:

IV. WRITE

Now write a **poem** of your own about the idea you chose. Use Tennyson's poem as a model.

1. Make your poem 8 lines long. Give it a title.
2. Repeat the same phrase in your first and second lines.
3. Even though poetry does not always follow grammatical rules, use the Writers' Checklist for ideas on how to revise.

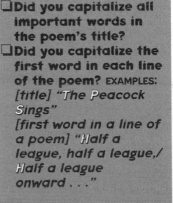

WRITERS' CHECK LIST

CAPITALIZATION

❏ Did you capitalize all important words in the poem's title?

❏ Did you capitalize the first word in each line of the poem? EXAMPLES: [title] "The Peacock Sings"
[first word in a line of a poem] "Half a league, half a league,/ Half a league onward . . ."

V. WRAP-UP

What did you like most—and what did you like least—about "The Charge of the Light Brigade"?

READERS' CHECKLIST

ENJOYMENT
- ☐ Did you like the reading?
- ☐ Was the reading experience pleasurable?
- ☐ Would you want to reread the piece or recommend it to someone?

Antarctica

Explorers never actually saw Antarctica until the early 1800s. Located at the South Pole, Antarctica is a land mass buried in more than 7,000 feet of ice. Only a few small plants and insects can survive there, and its freezing temperatures make human life nearly impossible.

15: Stuck Fast

What do you think of when you hear the word *Antarctica*? You probably picture ice, snow, or packs of dogs pulling sleds across the frozen ground. When Ernest Shackleton heard the word *Antarctica*, he thought "adventure" or "challenge." In 1914, he and a crew of 28 men sailed south to Antarctica. What follows is his story, as told in his autobiography *South*.

BEFORE YOU READ

Before you begin reading, preview the selection.
1. Work with a partner or a group of 2-3 other people.
2. Take turns reading these sentences from the selection.
3. Discuss what they tell you. Then try to answer the questions below.

PAIR AND SHARE

1. "But about 400 yds. of heavy ice, including old rafted pack, still separated the *Endurance* from the water, and reluctantly I had to admit that further effort was useless."

2. "The sun, which had been above the horizon for two months, set at midnight on the 17th, and, although it would not disappear until April, its slanting rays warned us of the approach of winter."

3. "I could not doubt now that the *Endurance* was confined for the winter."

4. "And will it be possible to break out of the pack early in the spring and reach Vahsel Bay or some other suitable landing-place?"

What did you learn about Shackleton's experience?

_____

_____

What can you tell about the continent of Antarctica?

_____

_____

What do you think will happen to Shackleton and his crew?

_____

_____

II. READ

Read through the selection at your own pace.
1. As you read, jot down any **questions** in the Response Notes.
2. Consider how Shackleton creates a feeling about what it was like in Antarctica.

"Stuck Fast" from *South* by Ernest Shackleton

NOTE: Ernest Shackleton's crew of 28 men set sail in their ship *Endurance* to the Antarctic. Not long after setting out, they were stuck fast between ice <u>floes</u>. They returned, barely, more than two years later after being pushed to the limits of their endurance.

The second half of February produced no important change in our situation. Early in the morning of the 14th I ordered a good head of steam on the engines and sent all hands on to the floe with ice-chisels, prickers, saws, and picks. We worked all day and throughout most of the next day in a <u>strenuous</u> effort to get the ship into the lead ahead. The men cut away the young ice before the bows and pulled it aside with great energy. After twenty-four hours' labor we had got the ship a third of the way to the lead. But about 400 yds. of heavy ice, including old rafted pack, still separated the *Enduranco* from tho water, and roluctantly I had to admit that further effort was useless.

RESPONSE NOTES

EXAMPLE:
If they'd been there two years were they scared?

STOP aND THiNK

What is Shackleton's crew trying to do?

_____

_____

_____

_____

VOCABULARY
floes—sheets of flowing ice.
strenuous—vigorous.

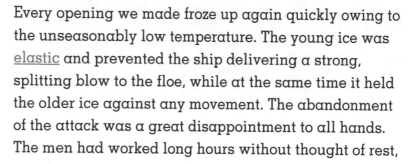

Every opening we made froze up again quickly owing to the unseasonably low temperature. The young ice was <u>elastic</u> and prevented the ship delivering a strong, splitting blow to the floe, while at the same time it held the older ice against any movement. The abandonment of the attack was a great disappointment to all hands. The men had worked long hours without thought of rest, and they deserved success. But the task was beyond our powers. I had not abandoned hope of getting clear, but was counting now on the possibility of having to spend a winter in the <u>inhospitable</u> arms of the pack. The sun, which had been above the horizon for two months, set at midnight on the 17th, and, although it would not disappear until April, its slanting rays warned us of the approach of winter. Pools and leads appeared occasionally, but they froze over very quickly.

stop and think

What forced the crew to give up?

_____

_____

_____

_____

VOCABULARY

elastic—capable of returning to its initial form.
inhospitable—unfriendly; hostile.

"Stuck Fast" CONTINUED

We continued to accumulate a supply of seal meat and blubber, and the <u>excursions</u> across the floes to shoot and bring in the seals provided welcome exercise for all hands. Three crab-eater cows shot on the 21st were not accompanied by a bull, and blood was to be seen about the hole from which they had crawled. We <u>surmised</u> that the bull had become the prey of one of the killer-whales. These aggressive creatures were to be seen often in the lanes and pools, and we were always distrustful of their ability or willingness to <u>discriminate</u> between seal and man. A lizard-like head would show while the killer gazed along the floe with wicked eyes. Then the brute would dive, to come up a few moments later, perhaps, under some unfortunate seal reposing on the ice. Worsley examined a spot where a killer had smashed a hole 8 ft. by 12 ft. in 12 ½ in. of hard ice, covered by 2½ in. of snow. Big blocks of ice had been tossed on to the floe surface. Wordie, engaged in measuring the thickness of young ice, went through to his waist one day just as a killer rose to blow in the adjacent lead. His companions pulled him out hurriedly.

stop and think

Why were the whales dangerous?

_____

_____

_____

VOCABULARY
excursions—short journeys.
surmised—guessed.
discriminate—differentiate.

RESPONSE NOTES

On the 22nd the *Endurance* reached the farthest south point of her drift, touching the 77th parallel of latitude in long. 35° W. The summer had gone; indeed the summer had scarcely been with us at all. The temperatures were low day and night, and the pack was freezing solidly around the ship. The thermometer recorded 10° below zero Fahr. at 2 a.m. on the 22nd. Some hours earlier we had watched a wonderful golden mist to the southward, where the rays of the declining sun shone through vapor rising from the ice. All normal standards of perspective vanish under such conditions, and the low ridges of the pack, with mist lying between them, gave the illusion of a wilderness of mountain-peaks like the Bernese Oberland. I could not doubt now that the *Endurance* was confined for the winter. Gentle breezes from the east, south, and south-west did not disturb the hardening floes. The seals were disappearing and the birds were leaving us. The land showed still in fair weather on the distant horizon, but it was beyond our reach now, and regrets for havens that lay behind us were vain.

VOCABULARY
77th parallel of latitude in long. 35° W—the exact location on the globe where Shackleton's ship, the *Endurance,* was stuck.
vapor—mist.
perspective—mental outlook; view.
illusion—false belief.
Bernese Oberland—range of mountains in Switzerland.
vain—useless.

ANTARCTICA

"Stuck Fast" CONTINUED

"We must wait for the spring, which may bring us better fortune. If I had guessed a month ago that the ice would grip us here, I would have established our base at one of the landing-places at the great <u>glacier</u>. But there seemed no reason to <u>anticipate</u> then that the <u>fates</u> would prove unkind. This calm weather with intense cold in a summer month is surely exceptional. My chief anxiety is the drift. Where will the <u>vagrant</u> winds and currents carry the ship during the long winter months that are ahead of us? We will go west, no doubt, but how far? And will it be possible to break out of the pack early in the spring and reach Vahsel Bay or some other suitable landing-place? These are momentous questions for us."

RESPONSE NOTES

VOCABULARY
glacier—large, slow-moving mass of ice.
anticipate—expect.
fates—superior forces. (In Greek mythology the fates control people's life spans.)
vagrant—ever changing; random.

stop and think

Summarize the biggest obstacles facing Shackleton and his crew.

_____

_____

_____

_____

How do his men feel about the difficulties they face?

_____

_____

_____

_____

GATHER YOUR THOUGHTS

A. DESCRIBE A PLACE Look back at the selection to note the way Shackleton describes Antarctica. List specific details he gives about each of the topics below.

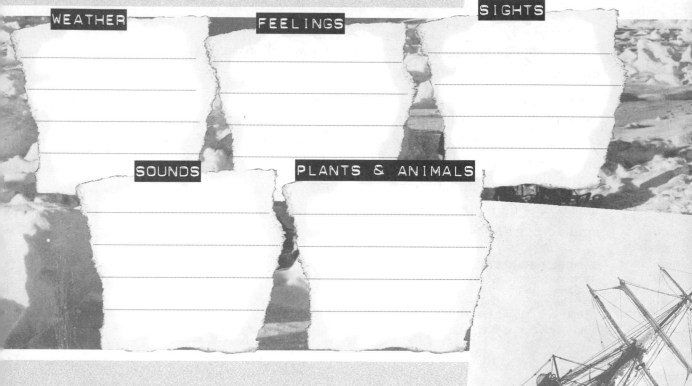

WEATHER

FEELINGS

SIGHTS

SOUNDS

PLANTS & ANIMALS

B. BUILD A DESCRIPTION Think of a place you have been to or have heard about. What kind of feeling would you want to create about it in a descriptive paragraph?

1. Start planning a descriptive paragraph by choosing a place.

2. Then use the web diagram below to note details about it.

FEELINGS

SOUNDS

The place I will describe is:

SIGHTS

WEATHER

PLANTS & ANIMALS

IV. WRITE

Now use your list of details to help you write a **descriptive paragraph**.

1. Start with a topic sentence that tells the place you are describing.
2. Then add details from your web to paint a picture of the place and to create a feeling about it.
3. Use the Writers' Checklist to help you revise your paragraph.

WRITERS' CHECKLIST

RUN-ON SENTENCES

☐ Did you check to see if you had any run-on sentences? If you join two sentences together to create a compound sentence, you need to use a comma and a conjunction, such as *and* or *but*. A compound sentence that is missing the joining word and the comma is a run-on. You can fix a run-on by adding the comma and conjunction or by breaking the run-on into two separate sentences. EXAMPLES:
The summer was gone the temperatures were low. (incorrect)
The summer was gone, and the temperatures were low. (correct)
The summer was gone. The temperatures were low. (correct)

V. WRAP-UP

What did you learn from reading this selection?

READERS' CHECKLIST

MEANING

- ❑ **Did you learn something from the reading?**
- ❑ **Did it affect you or make an impression?**

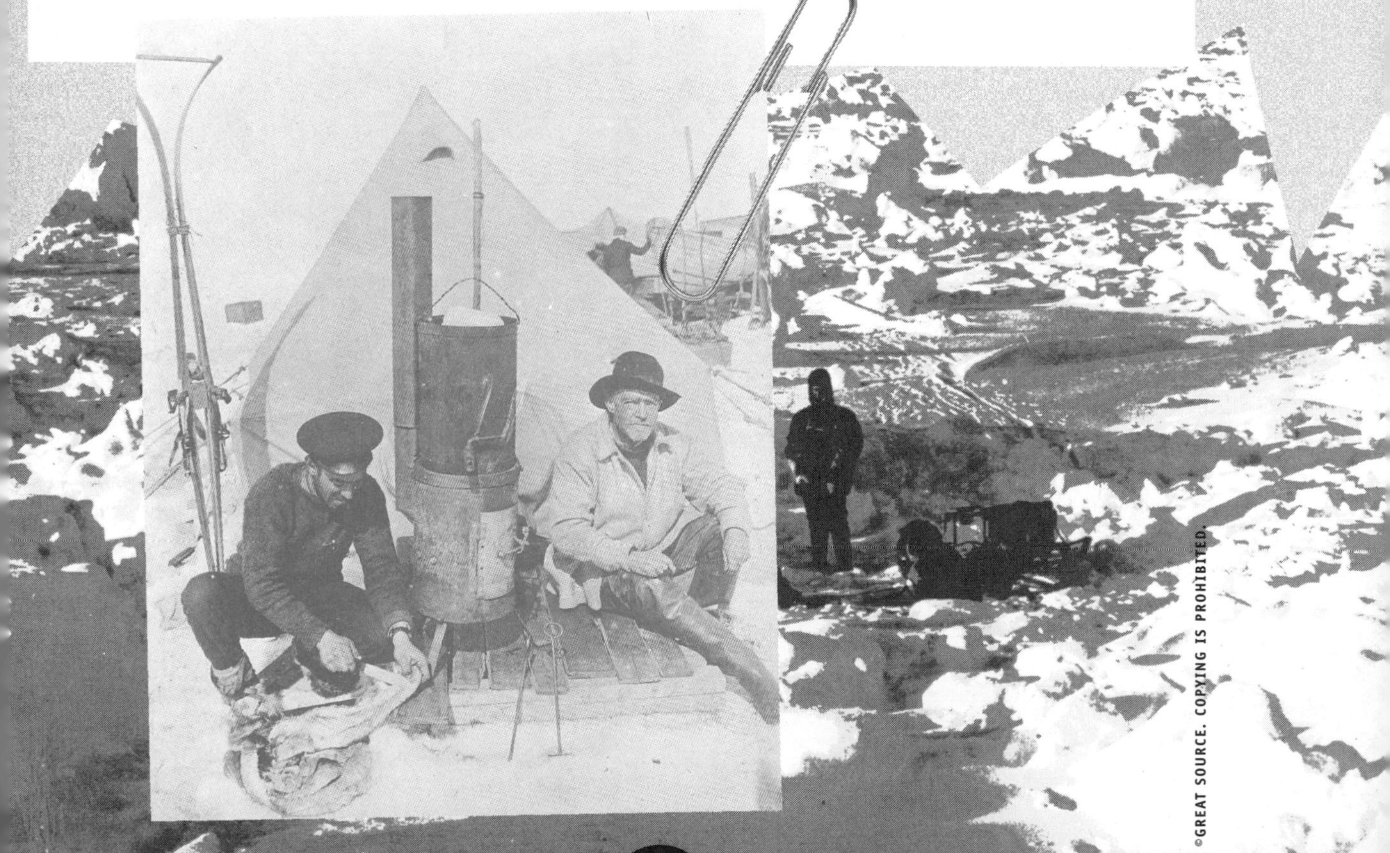

16: One Way Out

Did you ever hear the phrase "Never say never"? The story of Ernest Shackleton's return from Antarctica is almost too amazing to believe. His journey shows the limits of human endurance and why we should believe we can do anything if we set our minds to it.

BEFORE YOU READ

How can you get ready to read? You can prepare by thinking about what the selection is about.

1. Answer the questions in the Anticipation Guide below.

2. Then discuss your answers with a partner and make a prediction about what will happen.

ANTICIPATION GUIDE

AGREE DISAGREE

1. **When a ship gets stuck in ice in Antarctica, it's best to wait there on the ship until help arrives.**

2. **Traveling by ship more than 75 years ago was not very different from traveling by ship today.**

3. **A crew of 28 men could not survive if they had to camp on an iceberg in Antarctica for two years.**

4. **To survive in temperatures way below zero, you should sleep on the ground to get your body used to the cold.**

5. **Food is easy to find in Antarctica because of all the fish and seals.**

6. **A crew stuck for months in the ice and cold of Antarctica will turn against the captain of their ship.**

What do you think will happen to the crew of the <u>Endurance</u>?

_____

_____

_____

_____

II. READ

Read this excerpt from *Endurance*, a biography of Ernest Shackleton.

1. Think about how to **connect** Shackleton's experience to your own life.

2. Jot down your **reactions** to the selection in the Response Notes.

"One Way Out" by Alfred Lansing

RESPONSE NOTES

NOTE: Ernest Shackleton's crew of 28 men had to leave their ship *Endurance* in the Antarctic when they were stuck in the ice. To survive, he and his crew undertook an amazing and courageous journey. Everyone thought they had been lost, but all the men returned after a two-year journey that truly tested the limits of their endurance.

EXAMPLE:
I wonder if I would have stayed calm.

"May the Lord help you to do your duty & guide you through all the dangers by land and sea.

"May you see the Works of the Lord & all His Wonders in the deep."

These words were written on the <u>flyleaf</u> of a Bible given to the <u>expedition</u> by Queen Mother Alexandra of England. Shackleton carried the Bible in his hand as he left the *Endurance* and walked slowly across the ice toward the campsite.

The others hardly noticed his arrival. They were busy crawling in and out of the tents, trying, <u>numbly</u>, to create some degree of comfort with what energy remained in them. Some arranged pieces of lumber to keep themselves off the snow-covered ice. Others spread pieces of <u>canvas</u> as ground covers. But there was not enough flooring for everybody and several men had to lie directly on the bare snow. It made little difference. Sleep was all that mattered. And they slept—most of them embracing their nearest tentmates to keep from freezing.

VOCABULARY
flyleaf—blank sheet of paper at the beginning of a book.
expedition—journey for the purpose of exploration.
numbly—unable to feel or sense.
canvas—heavy, coarse fabric used for tents or sails.

©GREAT SOURCE. COPYING IS PROHIBITED.

"One Way Out" CONTINUED

Shackleton did not even try to sleep. He paced continually around the floe. The pressure was still intense, and several times the campsite <u>sustained</u> a violent <u>shock</u>. The dark outline of the *Endurance* 200 yards away rose against the clear night sky About 1 A.M., as Shackleton walked back and forth, there was a jolt; then a thin ribbon-like crack <u>snaked</u> across the floe among the tents. Almost immediately it began to widen. Shackleton hurried from tent to tent, waking the exhausted sleepers. It required an hour's tricky work in the dark to transfer the camp to the larger half of the floe.

Thereafter all was quiet in the camp, though just before dawn there was a loud report from the *Endurance*. Her bowsprit and jib boom had broken and dropped onto the ice. For the rest of the night, Shackleton could hear the ghostly rhythm of the chain from the <u>martingale</u> <u>boom</u> being slowly dragged back and forth by the movement of the ship.

STOP AND ORGANIZE

In the organizer below, write 3 things that have happened so far to the crew of the *Endurance*.

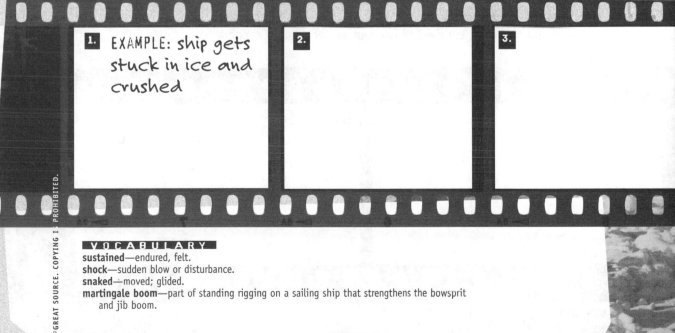

1. EXAMPLE: ship gets stuck in ice and crushed

2.

3.

VOCABULARY

sustained—endured, felt.
shock—sudden blow or disturbance.
snaked—moved; glided.
martingale boom—part of standing rigging on a sailing ship that strengthens the bowsprit and jib boom.

RESPONSE NOTES

When morning came, the weather was dull and overcast, but the temperature had climbed to 6 above zero. The men turned out stiff and cold from sleeping on the ice. It took a very long time for them to wake up. Shackleton did not press them, and after a time they turned to the job of sorting out equipment and stowing it securely on the sledges. It was a quiet time, and very few orders were given. Everyone understood his job and went about it without having to be told.

The plan, as they all knew, was to march toward Paulet Island, 346 miles to the northwest, where the stores left in 1902 should still be. The distance was farther than from New York City to Pittsburgh, Pennsylvania, and they would be dragging two of their three boats with them, since it was assumed that they would eventually run into open water.

McNeish and McLeod began mounting the whaler and one of the cutters onto sledges. The boats with their sledges would weigh more than a ton apiece, and nobody had any delusions that it would be easy to drag them over the chaotic surface of the ice, with its pressure ridges occasionally two stories high.

STOP AND ORGANIZE

What does the crew prepare to do? Write your answer in the first box. How will the crew survive? Write your answer in the second box.

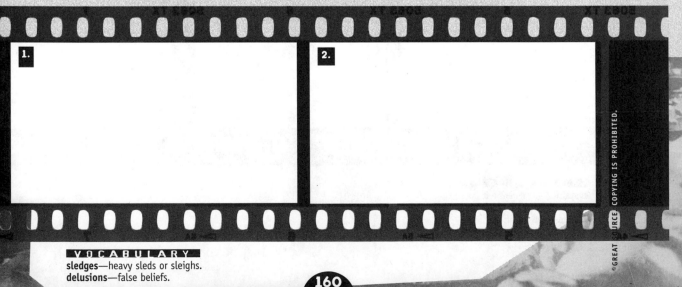

1.

2.

VOCABULARY
sledges—heavy sleds or sleighs.
delusions—false beliefs.

Nevertheless, there was a remarkable absence of discouragement. All the men were in a state of dazed fatigue, and nobody paused to reflect on the terrible consequences of losing their ship. Nor were they upset by the fact that they were now camped on a piece of ice perhaps 6 feet thick. It was a <u>haven</u> compared with the nightmare of labor and uncertainty of the last few days on the *Endurance*. It was quite enough to be alive—and they were merely doing what they had to do to stay that way.

There was even a trace of mild <u>exhilaration</u> in their attitude. At least, they had a clear-cut task ahead of them. The nine months of indecision, of speculation about what might happen, of aimless drifting with the pack were over. Now they simply had to get themselves out, however <u>appallingly</u> difficult that might be.

STOP AND ORGANIZE

Summarize the story of the *Endurance* in the organizer below.

1.

2.

3.

4.

5.

VOCABULARY
haven—place of rest.
exhilaration—energy.
appallingly—frightfully.

GATHER YOUR THOUGHTS

A. FIND THE MAIN IDEA When you answer the question, "What is the selection about?" you are telling the main idea.

1. Write the main idea of this selection in the top box.

2. Then write at least 4 details that explain more about that idea in the boxes below.

MAIN IDEA OF "ONE WAY OUT"

DETAIL	DETAIL	DETAIL	DETAIL

B. CHOOSE A SUBJECT Prepare to write a personal experience paragraph about a close-call or a frightening experience you had.

1. First, write the name of the experience you want to write about in the box labeled "Subject."

2. Then write a summary of 1–2 sentences that tells what you want to say about the experience.

SUBJECT:

C. DEVELOP YOUR SUBJECT Get ready to write your paragraph about a close-call or a frightening experience.

1. Walk through the event or experience step-by-step in your mind. Then in the boxes write 4 or 5 things that happened.
2. End with a concluding sentence that tells your overall feeling about the experience.

1.

2.

3.

5.

6.

4.

Overall feeling:

IV. WRITE

Now write a **personal experience paragraph** about your close-call or frightening experience.

1. Use your organizer on the previous page to help you tell the events in order.
2. Begin right before the most exciting part in the story. End with a sentence that makes clear your overall feeling.
3. Use the Writers' Checklist to help you revise.

WRITERS' CHECKLIST

SENTENCE FRAGMENTS

☐ Did you check to be sure your writing does not include any sentence fragments? Fragments are groups of words that lack complete subjects or complete verbs.

☞ If you have written a fragment that includes only a verb, add a subject.
INCORRECT: *Groups of men went back to the ship. Was packed in the ice.*
CORRECT: *Groups of men went back to the ship. It was packed in the ice.*

☞ If you have written a fragment that has only a subject, add a verb. INCORRECT: *The men were determined. A difficult task ahead.*
CORRECT: *The men were determined. A difficult task lay ahead.*

☞ If you have written a fragment without a subject or a verb, try combining it with another sentence.
INCORRECT: *The men camped. On the ice.*
CORRECT: *The men camped on the ice.*

Arthur C. Clarke

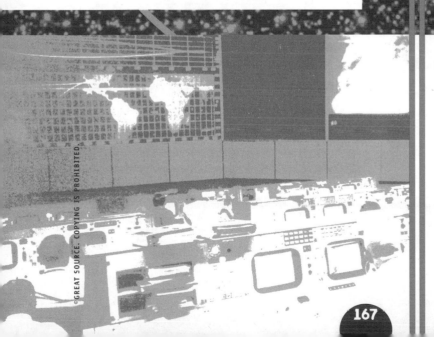

Arthur C. Clarke (1917–) was born in Somerset, England. Long fascinated by space and the planets and stars, he has mainly written science-fiction novels. Clarke also co-wrote the script for the popular movie, *2001: A Space Odyssey.*

What mood are you in? You can set the mood for reading the same way you set the mood for a party or anything else. When you get ready to read, block <u>out</u> distractions. Turn <u>on</u> your attention to the subject you're about to read.

BEFORE YOU READ

Read the title and first paragraph of the story on the next page.

1. Think about science-fiction stories you have read or movies you've seen. What might a brilliant scientist in a science-fiction story be like?

2. In a 1-minute quickwrite, write words and phrases that come to mind when you think about a brilliant scientist.

3. Share what you've written with the class.

Brilliant Scientist

QUICKWRITE

READ

Now finish reading the first part of "The Brilliant Konrad Schneider," the opening section of the novel *Childhood's End*.
1. Write any **questions** you have in the Response Notes.
2. As you read, circle the names of characters and interesting information about them.

"The Brilliant Konrad Schneider" from *Childhood's End* by Arthur C. Clarke

The Volcano that had reared Taratua up from the Pacific depths had been sleeping now for half a million years. Yet in a little while, thought Reinhold, the island would be bathed with fires fiercer than any that had attended its birth. He glanced towards the launching site, and his gaze climbed the pyramid of scaffolding that still surrounded the "Columbus." Two hundred feet above the ground, the ship's prow was catching the last rays of the descending sun. This was one of the last nights it would ever know: soon it would be floating in the eternal sunshine of space.

It was quiet here beneath the palms, high up on the rocky spine of the island. The only sound from the Project was the occasional yammering of an air compressor or the faint shout of a workman. Reinhold had grown fond of these clustered palms; almost every evening he had come here to survey his little empire. It saddened him to think that they would be blasted to atoms when the "Columbus" rose in flame and fury to the stars.

EXAMPLE:
Is Reinhold scared?

VOCABULARY

Taratua—island in the Pacific Ocean.
scaffolding—platform for holding workers and materials.
ship's prow—ship's frontal part.
air compressor—a mechanical device that forces air from one place to another.
atoms—tiny pieces of matter.

RESPONSE NOTES

A mile beyond the <u>reef</u>, the "James Forrestal" had switched on her searchlights and was sweeping the dark waters. The sun had now vanished completely, and the swift tropical night was racing in from the east. Reinhold wondered, a little <u>sardonically</u>, if the carrier expected to find Russian submarines so close to shore.

The thought of Russia turned his mind, as it always did, to Konrad and that morning in the <u>cataclysmic</u> spring of 1945. More than thirty years had passed, but the memory of those last days when the <u>Reich</u> was crumbling beneath the waves from the East and from the West had never faded.

STOP AND CLARIFY

Where and when does the story take place?

....

....

....

....

VOCABULARY
reef—strip of rocks that rises to the surface of a body of water.
sardonically—with scorn and disbelief.
cataclysmic—highly destructive.
Reich—German Nazi party that was in power during World War II.

"The Brilliant Konrad Schneider" continued

He could still see Konrad's tired blue eyes, and the golden stubble on his chin, as they shook hands and parted in that ruined Prussian village, while the refugees streamed endlessly past. It was a parting that symbolized everything that had since happened to the world—the cleavage between East and West. For Konrad chose the road to Moscow. Reinhold had thought him a fool, but now he was not so sure.

For thirty years he had assumed that Konrad was dead. It was only a week ago that Colonel Sandmeyer, of Technical Intelligence, had given him the news. He didn't like Sandmeyer, and he was sure the feeling was mutual. But neither let that interfere with business.

"Mr. Hoffmann," the Colonel had begun, in his best official manner, "I've just had some alarming information from Washington. It's top secret, of course, but we've decided to break it to the engineering staff so that they'll realize the necessity for speed." He paused for effect, but the gesture was wasted on Reinhold. Somehow, he already knew what was coming.

STOP AND PREDICT

What do you predict is coming?

....
....
....
....
....

VOCABULARY
stubble—short, rough growth.
Prussian—German. Prussia used to include present-day north Germany and Poland until it was abolished after World War II.
cleavage—split.
interfere—meddle; get in the way.

"The Russians are nearly level with us. They've got some kind of atomic drive—it may even be more efficient than ours, and they're building a ship on the shores of Lake Baikal. We don't know how far they've got, but Intelligence believes it may be launched this year. You know what *that* means."

Yes, thought Reinhold, I know. The race is on—and we may not win it.

"Do you know who's running their team?" he had asked, not really expecting an answer. To his surprise, Colonel Sandmeyer had pushed across a typewritten sheet and there at its head was the name: Konrad Schneider.

"You knew a lot of these men at Peenemünde, didn't you?" said the Colonel. "That may give us some insight into their methods. I'd like you to let me have notes on as many of them as you can—their specialties, the bright ideas they had, and so on. I know it's asking a lot after all this time—but see what you can do."

STOP AND QUESTION

What questions do you have about Konrad Schneider?

....

....

....

....

STOP AND QUESTION

"Konrad Schneider is the only one who matters," Reinhold had answered. "He was brilliant—the others are just <u>competent</u> engineers. Heaven only knows what he's done in thirty years. Remember—he's probably seen all our results and we haven't seen any of his. That gives him a decided advantage."

VOCABULARY
competent—sufficiently capable; qualified.

He hadn't meant this as a criticism of Intelligence, but for a moment it seemed as if Sandmeyer was going to be offended. Then the Colonel shrugged his shoulders.

"It works both ways—you've told me that yourself. Our free exchange of information means swifter progress, even if we do give away a few secrets. The Russian research departments probably don't know what their own people are doing half the time. We'll show them that Democracy can get to the moon first."

Democracy—Nuts! thought Reinhold, but knew better than to say it. One Konrad Schneider was worth a million names on an electoral-roll. And what had Konrad done by this time, with all the resources of the U.S.S.R. behind him? Perhaps, even now, his ship was already outward bound from Earth. . . .

V O C A B U L A R Y
electoral roll—election ballot.
resources—wealth and manpower.

SUMMARIZE SUMMARIZE SUMMARIZE SUMMARIZE SUMMARIZE

What did you learn about the characters Reinhold and Schneider?

....

....

....

....

....

How are they alike and how are they different?

similarities	differences
....	....
....	....
....	....
....	....

GATHER YOUR THOUGHTS

A. UNDERSTAND A CHARACTER Before you can write about a character, you need to gather all the information the author gives you.

1. Look back over what you wrote in the Response Notes and the parts of the selection you marked.

2. Then answer each of these questions about Konrad Schneider.

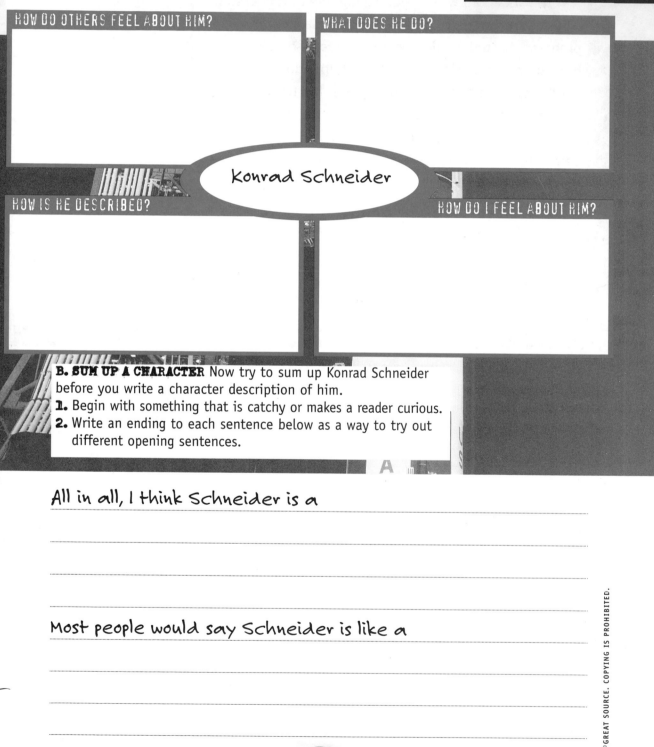

HOW DO OTHERS FEEL ABOUT HIM?

WHAT DOES HE DO?

Konrad Schneider

HOW IS HE DESCRIBED?

HOW DO I FEEL ABOUT HIM?

B. SUM UP A CHARACTER Now try to sum up Konrad Schneider before you write a character description of him.

1. Begin with something that is catchy or makes a reader curious.

2. Write an ending to each sentence below as a way to try out different opening sentences.

All in all, I think Schneider is a

Most people would say Schneider is like a

IV. WRITE

Now write a **character description** of Schneider.

1. Describe what you know and what you have inferred about him.

2. Begin with a strong, catchy sentence.

3. Use the Writers' Checklist to help you revise your paragraph.

WRITERS' CHECKLIST

COMMAS

☐ Did you use commas between clauses in a complex sentence? A complex sentence has a part that cannot stand alone (dependent clause) and one that can (independent clause).

EXAMPLE: *After you finish this book, you might pick up another Arthur C. Clarke book in the library.*

V. WRAP-UP

Would you say Clarke is a good writer?

READERS'
CHECKLIST

STYLE
☐ Did you find the passage well written?
☐ Are the sentences well constructed and the words well chosen?
☐ Does the style show you how to be a better writer?

18: The Brilliant Konrad Schneider continued

Who can tell what the future will bring? No one can "read" the future, but we all can look ahead and guess what will happen next.

BEFORE YOU READ

Get together with a partner or in a small group.
1. Read each prediction. Decide if you agree or not.
2. Put a check mark in either the "will happen" or "will not happen" column of the Anticipation Guide.
3. After you have finished, discuss your predictions with your partner or group.

PREDICTION	WILL HAPPEN	WILL NOT HAPPEN
1. Reinhold and Konrad Schneider will meet and have an argument.		
2. Reinhold will become disgusted and quit the project.		
3. Something will go wrong with the "Columbus."		
4. The Russians will launch first.		
5. The Americans will launch first.		
6. Both will launch at the same time.		
7. Neither group will launch.		

ANTICIPATION GUIDE

Now read the second part of Arthur Clarke's "The Brilliant Konrad Schneider."

1. Recall what has happened in the story up to this point. Note in the storyboard below at least 3 things that have happened so far.

2. Then read the selection and **mark or highlight** the sequence of other events in the Response Notes.

WHAT 3 THINGS HAVE HAPPENED IN THE STORY SO FAR?

1.

2.

3.

"The Brilliant Konrad Schneider" (continued) from *Childhood's End* by Arthur C. Clarke

RESPONSE NOTES

EXAMPLE:
motor test finished

The sun which had deserted Taratua was still high above Lake Baikal when Konrad Schneider and the Assistant Commissar for Nuclear Science walked slowly back from the motor test rig. Their ears were still throbbing painfully, though the last thunderous echoes had died out across the lake ten minutes before.

"Why the long face?" asked Grigorievitch suddenly. "You should be happy now. In another month we'll be on our way, and the Yankees will be choking themselves with rage."

VOCABULARY
motor test rig—testing ship.
Yankees—Americans.

"The Brilliant Konrad Schneider" continued

"You're an <u>optimist</u>, as usual," said Schneider. "Even though the motor works, it's not as easy as that. True, I can't see any serious obstacles now—but I'm worried about the reports from Taratua. I've told you how good Hoffmann is, and he's got billions of dollars behind him. Those photographs of his ship aren't very clear, but it looks as if it's not far from completion. And we know he tested his motor five weeks ago."

"Don't worry," laughed Grigorievitch. *"They're* the ones who are going to have the big surprise. Remember—they don't know a thing about us."

STOP AND RETELL STOP AND RETELL STOP AND RETELL

1. Where has the action of the story shifted?

2. What are Schneider and the Russians planning?

Schneider wondered if that was true, but decided it was much safer to express no doubts. That might start Grigorievitch's mind exploring far too many <u>tortuous</u> <u>channels</u>, and if there had been a leak, he would find it hard enough to clear himself.

VOCABULARY
optimist—someone who is positive and looks on the bright side of things.
tortuous—complex.
channels—routes. (In this instance, Clarke means ideas.)

The guard saluted as he re-entered the administration building. There were nearly as many soldiers here, he thought grimly, as technicians. But that was how the Russians did things, and as long as they kept out of his way he had no complaints. On the whole—with <u>exasperating</u> exceptions—events had turned out very much as he had hoped. Only the future could tell if he or Reinhold had made the better choice.

He was already at work on his final report when the sound of shouting voices disturbed him. For a moment he sat motionless at his desk, wondering what <u>conceivable</u> event could have disturbed the rigid discipline of the camp. Then he walked to the window—and for the first time in his life he knew <u>despair</u>.

STOP AND RETELL STOP AND RETELL STOP AND RETELL

1. What does Schneider hear?

2. How does Schneider feel?

The stars were all around him as Reinhold descended the little hill. Out at sea, the "Forrestal" was still sweeping the water with her fingers of light, while

VOCABULARY
exasperating—annoying.
conceivable—possible; understandable.
despair—hopelessness.

"The Brilliant Konrad Schneider" continued

further along the beach the scaffolding round the "Columbus" had transformed itself into an <u>illuminated</u> Christmas tree. Only the projecting prow of the ship lay like a dark shadow across the stars.

A radio was blaring dance music from the living quarters, and unconsciously Reinhold's feet <u>accelerated</u> to the rhythm. He had almost reached the narrow road along the edge of the sands when some <u>premonition</u>, some half movement, made him stop. <u>Puzzled</u>, he glanced from land to sea and back again: it was some little time before he thought of looking at the sky.

Then Reinhold Hoffmann knew, as did Konrad Schneider at this same moment, that he had lost his race. And he knew that he had lost it, not by the few weeks or months that he had feared, but by <u>millennia</u>.

The huge and silent shadows driving across the stars, more miles above his head than be dared to guess, were as far beyond his little "Columbus" as it surpassed the log canoes of <u>Paleolithic</u> man. For a moment that seemed to last forever, Reinhold watched, as all the world was watching, while the great ships descended in their overwhelming <u>majesty</u> until at last he could hear the faint scream of their passage through the thin air of the <u>stratosphere</u>.

He felt no regrets as the work of a lifetime was swept away. He had labored to take man to the stars, and, in the moment of success, the stars—the <u>aloof</u>, <u>indifferent</u> stars—had come to him. This was the moment when history held its breath, and the present

VOCABULARY
illuminated—brightly lit.
accelerated—sped up.
premonition—bad feeling.
Puzzled—confused.
millennia—thousands of years.
Paleolithic—period beginning 750,000 years ago and ending 15,000 years ago.
majesty—greatness and dignity.
stratosphere—upper atmosphere.
aloof—emotionally and physically distant.
indifferent—unbiased; neutral.

RESPONSE NOTES

<u>sheared asunder</u> from the past as an iceberg splits from its frozen, parent cliffs, and goes sailing out to sea in lonely pride. All that the past ages had achieved was as nothing now: only one thought echoed and re-echoed through Reinhold's brain:

The human race was no longer alone.

VOCABULARY
sheared asunder—cut apart.

Retell the whole story about Konrad Schneider using the 6 storyboard boxes below.
1. Start at the beginning of the story on page 169.
2. Show the sequence of 6 main events. Put only 1 event in each box.

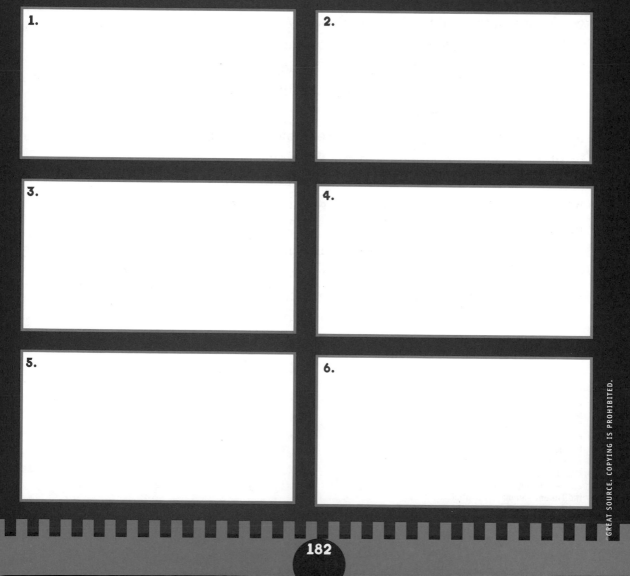

STOP AND RETELL STOP AND RETELL STOP AND RETELL

1.

2.

3.

4.

5.

6.

GATHER YOUR THOUGHTS

A. DEVELOP AN OPINION After you read, try to sort out your opinions from those of the writer and the characters.

1. In the "My Views" column, write your answer to each question.

QUESTIONS	MY VIEWS
DOES LIFE EXIST IN OUTER SPACE?	
HAVE ALIENS EVER LANDED ON EARTH?	
DO YOU BELIEVE IN UFOS (UNIDENTIFIED FLYING OBJECTS)?	

2. Complete this sentence to create a thesis for a persuasive paragraph:

My opinion of life on other planets is . . .

B. IDENTIFY SOURCES To be persuasive, a thesis must be supported by a variety of facts, opinions, and examples.

1. Think about where you could find information about life on other planets.

2. List 2-3 sources, people, or references you could use to find information to support your thesis.

EXPERT OPINIONS

NEWS ARTICLES OR MAGAZINES

FACTS

PEOPLE'S PERSONAL EXPERIENCES

C. RESEARCH Use your notes on the previous page to help you research the topic of life on other planets.

1. You may want to go to the library or use the Internet to find material.

2. Jot at least 1 item in each box to help you support your thesis about life on other planets.

Thesis:

Opinion of an expert (like a scientist):

Quote from news article or magazine:

Facts that support your opinion:

People's personal experiences:

IV. WRITE

Now write a **persuasive paragraph** about your opinion of life on other planets.

1. Begin with a topic sentence that develops your thesis.

2. Use the research material you gathered to support your thesis.

3. Use the Writers' Checklist to help you revise your paragraph.

WRITERS' CHECKLIST

USAGE

☐ Did you use *your* and *you're* correctly? *Your* is a possessive pronoun used to show ownership. *You're* is the contraction for *you are.* EXAMPLES: *Your dinner is ready. You're already behind schedule.*

☐ Did you use *affect* and *effect* correctly? *Affect* is always a verb; it means "to influence." *Effect* can be a verb, but it is most often used as a noun. As a noun, *effect* means "the result." EXAMPLES: *Teresa's laughter affected the whole class. I hope my essay will have a strong effect on readers.*

Continue your writing on the next page.

Continue your writing on the next page.

WRAP-UP

What did Arthur C. Clarke's story make you think about?

Families

Families bind people together through blood and love. They shape what we think and how we act. They make us feel loved and safe. But sometimes families have their own troubles.

How do our families shape us? How do they affect the persons we become? Charles Wadsworth once said, "By the time a man realizes that maybe his father was right, he usually has a son who thinks he's wrong." Is there any truth to that statement?

BEFORE YOU READ

When you hear the word *father*, what comes to mind? (If you want, use the word *mother* instead.)

1. Complete the Character Map. Write the word *fathers* or *mothers* in the middle box.

2. In the other spaces, jot down your ideas about fathers or mothers.

Character Map

1. Words they use:

2. Who they are like:

3. Things they do:

4. What's important to them:

5. How I feel about them:

READ

Read this part of J. M. Coetzee's autobiography at your own pace.
1. As you begin reading, try to **predict** how the writer will react to his father.
2. In the Response Notes, write your thoughts about the father.

"Father" from *Boyhood* by J. M. Coetzee

He has never worked out the position of his father in the household. In fact, it is not obvious to him by what right his father is there at all. In a normal household, he is prepared to accept, the father stands at the head: the house belongs to him, the wife and children live under his <u>sway</u>. But in their own case, and in the households of his mother's two sisters as well, it is the mother and children who make up the core, while the husband is no more than an <u>appendage</u>, a contributor to the economy as a paying <u>lodger</u> might be.

As long as he can remember he has had a sense of himself as prince of the house, and of his mother as his <u>dubious</u> promoter and anxious protector—anxious, dubious because, he knows, a child is not meant to rule the <u>roost</u>. If there is anyone to be jealous of, it is not his father but his younger brother. For his mother promotes his brother too—promotes and even, because his brother is clever but not as clever as he, nor as bold or adventurous, favors him. In fact, his mother seems always to be hovering over his brother, ready to <u>ward</u> off danger; whereas in his own case she is only somewhere in the background, waiting, listening, ready to come if he should call.

He wants her to behave toward him as she does toward his brother. But he wants this as a sign, a proof,

EXAMPLE:
Because Coetzee uses the word "normal," I think his father will be strange.

VOCABULARY
sway—influence.
appendage—something added or attached to a more important part.
lodger—person who rents and lives in a furnished room.
dubious—uncertain; doubtful.
roost—household.
ward—fight.

no more. He knows that he will fly into a rage if she ever begins hovering over him.

He keeps driving her into corners, demanding that she admit whom she loves more, him or his brother. Always she slips the trap. "I love you both the same," she maintains, smiling. Even his most <u>ingenious</u> questions—what if the house were to catch fire, for instance, and she had time to rescue only one of them?—fail to <u>snare</u> her.

"Both of you," she says, "I will surely save both of you."

"But the house won't catch fire." Though he mocks her for her <u>literal-mindedness</u>, he respects her <u>dogged constancy</u>.

His rages against his mother are one of the things he has to keep a careful secret from the world outside. Only the four of them know what <u>torrents</u> of scorn he pours upon her, how much like an inferior he treats her. 'If your teachers and your friends knew how you spoke to your mother . . . ,' says his father, wagging a finger meaningfully. He hates his father for seeing so clearly the chink in his armor.

stop+reflect

Who is "he" and how does he feel about his father?

| VOCABULARY |
ingenious—clever.
snare—trick.
literal-mindedness—reading everything word-for-word; not looking below the surface of words or things.
dogged—stubborn.
constancy—nonchanging personality.
torrents—heavy streams.

"Father" continued

He wants his father to beat him and turn him into a normal boy. At the same time he knows that if his father dared to strike him, he would not rest until he had his revenge. If his father were to hit him, he would go mad: he would become possessed, like a rat in a corner, <u>hurtling</u> about, snapping with its poisonous fangs, too dangerous to be touched.

At home he is an <u>irascible</u> <u>despot</u>, at school a lamb, <u>meek and mild</u>, who sits in the second row from the back, the most <u>obscure</u> row, so that he will not be noticed, and goes <u>rigid</u> with fear when the beating starts. By living this double life he has created for himself a burden of <u>imposture</u>. No one else has to bear anything like it, not even his brother, who is at most a nervous <u>wishy-washy</u> imitation of himself. In fact, he suspects that at heart his brother may be normal. He is on his own. From no quarter can he expect support. It is up to him to somehow get beyond childhood, beyond family and school, to a new life where he will not need to pretend any more.

stop+reflect

How would you describe the person referred to only as "he"?

_____

_____

_____

stop+reflect

VOCABULARY
hurtling—moving quickly.
irascible—easily angered.
despot—ruler with absolute power.
meek and mild—gentle and kind.
obscure—not well-known.
rigid—stiff.
imposture—deception.
wishy-washy—weak; not strong or decisive.

"Father" continued

Childhood, says the *Children's Encyclopedia*, is a time of innocent joy, to be spent in the meadows amid buttercups and bunny-rabbits or at the <u>hearthside</u> absorbed in a storybook. It is a vision of childhood utterly <u>alien</u> to him. Nothing he experiences in Worcester, at home or at school, leads him to think that childhood is anything but a time of gritting the teeth and enduring.

VOCABULARY
hearthside—fireplace.
alien—unknown; strange.

stop+reflect

How do you feel about the statement that childhood is nothing "but a time of gritting the teeth and enduring"?

In what way does this story connect with your life?

GATHER YOUR THOUGHTS

A. NARROW A TOPIC The subject of family is big and broad. The writer narrowed the subject to write about just one small part of that subject. Try to do the same with your subject.

1. Study the example.
2. Then narrow the subject of family for an autobiographical paragraph you will write.

EXAMPLE:

family
BROAD TOPIC

our holiday celebrations
NARROW

my akwardness at July 4th picnics
NARROWER

BROAD TOPIC

NARROW

NARROWER

B. DEVELOP A PARAGRAPH Before you write about an experience, it helps to recall specific details.

1. Think about the narrowed topic you wrote above. Choose a related experience you had that was important to you. Write it in the center circle.
2. Then explore that experience, using the graphic organizer to develop exactly what happened and how you felt about it.

1. How my family felt about it

2. Why it was important to me

3. What it says about our family

4. What it tells about me

IV. WRITE

Now write an **autobiographical paragraph.**

1. Start with a sentence that introduces when and where the experience took place.
2. Then explore how you and others in your family felt about the experience.
3. End with a sentence that tells why the experience was meaningful.
4. Use the Writers' Checklist below to help you revise.

V. WRAP-UP

How did this selection affect you? What impression did it make on you?

How would you describe your childhood? Writers often write about what their lives were like as children. Looking backward after many years, they tell about the experiences they were unable to explain when they were so young.

BEFORE YOU READ

Take a moment to preview Sui Sin Far's memoir about growing up.
1. Read the title and first paragraph below.
2. Then answer the questions on the Preview Card as best you can.

"Mama Is Chinese" from *Leaves from the Mental Portfolio of an Eurasian*
by Sui Sin Far (Edith Maud Eton)

When I look back over the years I see myself, a little child of scarcely four years of age, walking in front of my nurse, in a green English lane, and listening to her tell <u>another of her kind</u> that my mother is Chinese. "Oh, Lord!" exclaims the informed. She turns me around and scans me curiously from head to foot. Then the two women whisper together. Tho the word "Chinese" conveys very little meaning to my mind, I feel that they are talking about my father and mother and my heart swells with <u>indignation</u>. When we reach home I rush to my mother and try to tell her what I have heard. I am a young child. I fail to make myself <u>intelligible</u>. My mother does not understand, and when the nurse declares to her, "Little Miss Sui is a story-teller," my mother slaps me.

VOCABULARY
another of her kind—another nurse.
indignation—anger or rage.
intelligible—understandable or clear.

Preview Card

What does this title suggest to you?

What do you predict Sui Sin Far's childhood will be like?

II. READ

Read the rest of Sui Sin Far's memoir at your own pace.
1. As you read, ask yourself, "What kind of person is she? How does she feel about these experiences?"
2. Note your own **reactions** and **connections** to her story in the Response Notes.

"Mama Is Chinese" continued

Many a long year has past over my head since that day—the day on which I first learned that I was something different and apart from other children, but tho my mother has forgotten it, I have not.

I see myself again, a few years older. I am playing with another child in a garden. A girl passes by outside the gate. "Mamie," she cries to my companion. "I wouldn't speak to Sui if I were you. Her mama is Chinese."

"I don't care," answers the little one beside me. And then to me, "Even if your mamma is Chinese, I like you better than I like Annie."

"But I don't like you," I answer, turning my back on her. It is my first conscious lie.

Response Notes

EXAMPLE:
like how I felt I didn't fit in in elementary school

I am at a children's party, given by the wife of an <u>Indian officer</u> whose children were schoolfellows of mine. I am only six years of age, but have attended a private school for over a year, and have already learned that China is a <u>heathen</u> country, being <u>civilized</u> by England. However, for the time being, I am a merry <u>romping</u> child. There are quite a number of grown people present. One, a white haired old man, has his attention called to me by the hostess. He adjusts his eyeglasses and <u>surveys</u> me critically. "Ah, indeed!" he exclaims, "Who would have thought it at first glance. Yet now I see the difference between her and other children. What a peculiar coloring! Her mother's eyes and hair and her father's features, I presume. Very interesting little creature!"

I had been called from my play for the purpose of <u>inspection</u>. I do not return to it. For the rest of the evening I hide myself behind a hall door and refuse to show myself until it is time to go home.

stop+reflect

What two experiences has she told about?

1.

2.

How does she feel after them?

stop+reflect

VOCABULARY
Indian officer—government official in the country of India during British rule.
heathen—uncivilized.
civilized—advanced in social customs; well-bred and having good manners.
romping—playing in a rough, loud, fun-loving way.
surveys—looks over.
inspection—act of looking over slowly and carefully.

My parents have come to America. We are in Hudson City, N.Y., and we are very poor. I am out with my brother, who is ten months older than myself. We pass a Chinese store, the door of which is open. "Look!" says Charlie, "Those men in there are Chinese!" Eagerly I gaze into the long low room. With the exception of my mother, who is English bred with English ways and manner of dress, I have never seen a Chinese person. The two men within the store are uncouth specimens of their race, dressed in working blouses and pantaloons with queues hanging down their backs. I recoil with a sense of shock.

"Oh, Charlie," I cry, "Are we like that?"

"Well, we're Chinese, and they're Chinese, too, so we must be!" returns my seven-year-old brother.

VOCABULARY
uncouth specimens—rough and rude people.
blouses—loose-fitting shirts .
pantaloons—tight-fitting pants.
queues—braids of hair.

Summarize

Summarize in your own words what the 2 children felt as they looked in the Chinese store.

....

....

....

....

....

....

....

....

....

中港百貨
CENTRAL PORT
EMPORIUM GIFT SHOP
● 日用百貨
● 兒童玩具
● 各種吊飾
● 精工藝品
代理
中國唱片公司 CD - VCD LD 卡式盒帶
無線　錄影帶　亞視　錄影帶出租

CHINESE MUSIC
SOUVENIRS
GINSENG
BEANIE BABIES

A. USE A CLUSTER When writers write about their lives, they carefully select which parts to relate.

1. Study the example of how Sui Sin Far might have arrived at the experiences she wrote about.

2. Then use a similar cluster to develop ideas about an experience you might write about.

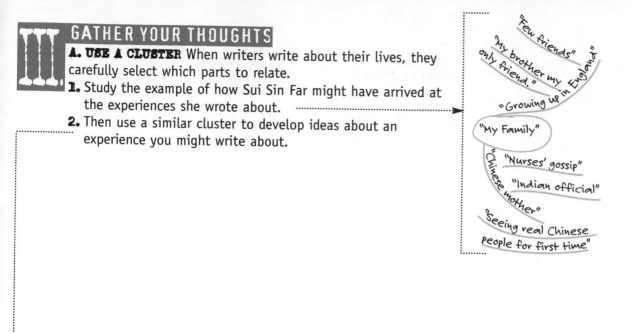

"Few friends"

"My brother my only friend."

"up in England"

"Growing up"

"My Family"

"Nurses' gossip"

"Indian official"

"Chinese mother"

"Seeing real Chinese people for first time"

B. QUICKWRITE Pick 1 of the small topics in your cluster.

1. Spend 1 minute quickwriting about the topic.

2. Try to write as much as you can without stopping. Then look over what you wrote.

3. Put a star by the particular experiences you want to write about in part of your autobiography.

Quickwrite

Topic:

IV. WRITE

Now write part of your **autobiography**, telling about some experiences in your life.

1. If you want, begin like Sui Sin Far: "When I look back over the years, I see myself. . . ."
2. Write about the experiences you developed in your quickwriting on the previous page. Put each experience in a separate paragraph.
3. Use the Writers' Checklist to help you revise.

WRITERS' CHECKLIST

POSSESSIVES

☐ Did you remember to use apostrophes with possessive nouns?

✔ Use an apostrophe and s to form the possessive of a singular noun, even one that ends in s. EXAMPLES: *the child's parents, the bus's wheels*

✔ Use an apostrophe alone to form the possessive of plural nouns ending in s. EXAMPLES: *the girls' words, the countries' people*

✔ Use an apostrophe and s to form the possessive of a plural noun that does not end in s. EXAMPLE: *the children's memory, the men's shirts*

Continue your writing on the next page.

Continue your writing from the previous page.

V. WRAP-UP

What in your own words is Sui Sin Far's memoir about?

The Written Word

The earliest system of writing dates back more than 5,500 years. Since then, people have used writing to communicate with others, express opinions, and entertain. Writing remains an essential part of life that no amount of technology will ever replace.

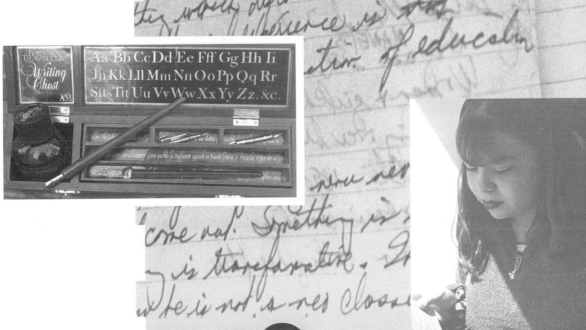

What do you know about writing? Have you ever wondered how authors learn to write? Here's your chance to learn. C. S. Lewis, author of *The Lion, the Witch, and the Wardrobe,* has some plain, no-nonsense advice: writing takes practice.

I.
BEFORE YOU READ

Think about all the rules you've ever heard about writing. Which have been most useful to you?

1. List them in the **K** space below.

2. Next think about what you want to know about writing. Write your questions in the **W** space.

3. After you read, come back to the **L** space and write what you have learned about writing.

K–W–L CHART

K What I **K**now

W What I **W**ant to Know

L What I **L**earned

II. READ

Now read C. S. Lewis's letter.

1. Mark or **highlight** any information that might answer the questions you wrote in your K-W-L Chart.

2. Put stars next to any advice that you think is particularly good.

"C. S. Lewis to a Schoolgirl" by C. S. Lewis

To a schoolgirl in America, who had written (at her teacher's suggestion) to request advice on writing.

14 December 1959

It is very hard to give any general advice about writing. Here's my attempt.

(1) Turn off the radio.

(2) Read all the good books you can, and avoid nearly all magazines.

(3) Always write (and read) with the ear, not the eye. You should hear every sentence you write as if it was being read aloud or spoken. If it does not sound nice, try again.

RESPONSE NOTES

EXAMPLE:
Avoid distractions. Need to be able to concentrate on sound.

STOP AND CLARIFY

What does Lewis mean to "write (and read) with the ear, not the eye"?

(4) Write about what really interests you, whether it is real things or imaginary things, and nothing else. (Notice this means that if you are interested *only* in writing, you will never be a writer, because you will have nothing to write about. . . .)

(5) Take great pains to be *clear*. Remember that though you start by knowing what you mean, the reader doesn't, and a single ill-chosen word may lead him to a total misunderstanding. In a story it is terribly easy just to forget that you have not told the reader something that he wants to know—the whole picture is so clear in your own mind that you forget that it isn't the same in his.

(6) When you give up a bit of work don't (unless it is hopelessly bad) throw it away. Put it in a drawer. It may come in useful later. Much of my best work, or what I think is my best, is the re-writing of things begun and <u>abandoned</u> years earlier.

(7) Don't use a typewriter. The noise will destroy your sense of rhythm, which still needs years of training.

(8) Be sure you know the meaning (or meanings) of every word you use.

STOP AND QUESTION

What questions do you have about this advice for writing?

....

....

....

Which of these rules seem to you to be most important? Why?

....

....

....

VOCABULARY
abandoned—set aside and forgotten.

Return to the K-W-L Chart on page 204. Write what you learned in the **L** space.

GATHER YOUR THOUGHTS

A. BRAINSTORM Imagine you've been asked to advise someone a little younger than you on how to be a good reader. What advice can you give in a letter?

1. Brainstorm a list of 8-10 tips here.

2. When you've finished, discuss your list with a partner.

1.

2.

3.

4.

5.

6.

7.

8.

9.

10.

TIPS FOR READERS

B. PLAN YOUR LETTER Make some planning notes for your letter about how to be a good reader.

1. First plan an introduction, stating the purpose of your letter.

2. Then draft the advice you will give in the main body of the letter. Use your brainstorming list for ideas.

3. Last, close with some encouraging words and something about your own experiences about improving your reading skills.

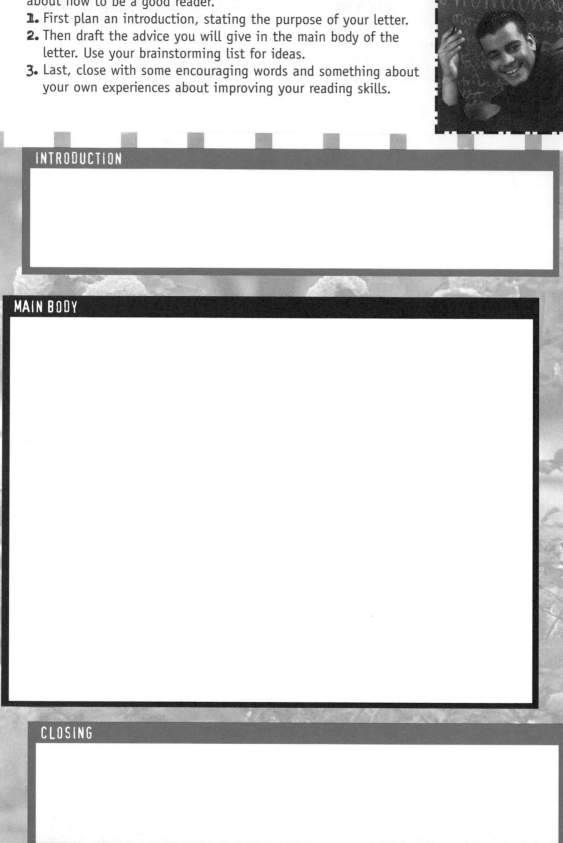

INTRODUCTION

MAIN BODY

CLOSING

IV. WRITE

Now write a **letter** advising someone a little younger than you
on ways to improve his or her reading.

1. Use your planning notes to help you include an introduction,
a body, and a conclusion.

2. Use the Writers' Checklist to help you revise your letter.

Continue your writing on the next page.

WRITERS' CHECKLIST

LETTERS

❑ Did you place a comma at the end of a greeting of a friendly letter? EXAMPLE: *Dear Mitchell,*

❑ Did you use a comma after the day in the date? EXAMPLE: *April 17,*

❑ Did you use a comma after the closing of a friendly letter? EXAMPLE: *Sincerely,*

Continue your writing from the previous page.

WRAP-UP

Was the advice by C.S. Lewis worth reading? Explain.

22: The Need to Say It

Do you take the time to "read" pictures? Look at the art or photos with a selection carefully. Read each caption closely. By taking a picture walk before you read, you can gain a quick impression of what will follow. The pictures will give you a frame of reference that can help you understand what you read.

BEFORE YOU READ

Look at the pictures throughout the following essay. Read the captions that go with them.

1. Choose 3 of your favorite photographs and record your ideas on the chart.

2. Then make a prediction about the selection.

The photo of . . .	tells me . . .
1.	
2.	
3.	

Based on the photos, I predict "The Need to Say It" will be about . . .

PICTURE WALK

READ

Now read Patricia Hampl's essay.

1. Try to **visualize** the scene she describes.

2. Make sketches or drawings of details that interest or surprise you.

EXAMPLE:

"The Need to Say It" by Patricia Hampl

My Czech grandmother hated to see me with a book. She snatched it away if I sat still too long (dead to her), absorbed in my reading. "Bad for you," she would say, holding the <u>loathsome</u> thing behind her back, furious at my <u>enchantment</u>.

She kept her distance from the printed word of English, but she <u>lavished</u> attention on her lodge newspaper which came once a month, written in the quaint nineteenth-century Czech she and her generation had brought to America before the turn of the century. Like wedding cake saved from the feast, this language, over the years, had become a <u>fossil</u>, still recognizable but no longer something to be put in the mouth.

Czech newspapers

Did she read English? I'm not sure. I do know that she couldn't—or didn't—write it. That's where I came in.

STOP AND CLARIFY

How does the grandmother feel about reading?

....

....

....

....

STOP AND CLARIFY

VOCABULARY

loathsome—hateful.
enchantment—spell-binding interest.
lavished—gave much.
fossil—part of the past.

My first commissioned work was to write letters for her. "You write for me, honey?" she would say, holding out a ball point she had been given at a grocery store promotion, clicking it like a castanet. My fee was cookies and milk, payable before, during, and after completion of the project.

I settled down at her kitchen table while she rooted around the drawer where she kept coupons and playing cards and bank calendars. Eventually she located a piece of stationery and a mismatched envelope. She laid the small, pastel sheet before me, smoothing it out; a floral motif was clotted across the top of the page and bled down one side. The paper was so insubstantial even ball-point ink seeped through to the other side. "That's okay," she would say. "We only need one side."

A young woman writing

True. In life she was a gifted gossip, unfurling an extended riff of chatter from a bare motif of rumor. But her writing style displayed a brevity that made Hemingway's prose look like nattering garrulity. She dictated her letters as if she were paying by the word.

VOCABULARY
commissioned—authorized; professional.
castanet—rhythm instrument held in the hand.
rooted—dug; searched.
pastel—soft colored; pale.
floral motif—flower design.
clotted—grouped; lumped together.
insubstantial—thin and of poor quality.
unfurling—spreading.
riff—phrase.
brevity—briefness.
nattering garrulity—excessive talk or chatter.
dictated—said aloud.

"Dear Sister," she began, followed by a little time-buying cough and throat-clearing. "We are all well here." Pause. "And hope you are well too." Longer pause, the steamy broth of inspiration heating up on her side of the table. Then, in a <u>lurch</u>, "Winter is hard so I don't get out much."

This was followed instantly by an <u>unconquerable</u> fit of <u>envy</u>: "Not like you in California." Then she came to a complete halt, perhaps <u>demoralized</u> by this evidence that you can't put much on paper before you betray your secret self, try as you will to keep things <u>civil</u>.

She sat, she <u>brooded</u>, she stared out the window. She was locked in the <u>perverse</u> <u>reticence</u> of <u>composition</u>. She gazed at me, but I understood she did not see me. She was looking for her next thought. "Read what I wrote," she would finally say, having lost not only what she was looking for but what she already had pinned down. I went over the little trail of sentences that led to her dead end.

More silence, then a sigh. She gave up the ghost. "Put 'God bless you,'" she said. She reached across to see the lean rectangle of words on the paper. "Now leave some space," she said, "and put 'Love.'"

STOP AND QUESTION

What questions would you like to ask about the letters?

....

....

....

....

VOCABULARY
lurch—sudden movement.
unconquerable—unbeatable.
envy—jealousy.
demoralized—disheartened; discouraged.
civil—polite.
brooded—thought deeply.
perverse—cranky.
reticence—unwillingness.
composition—writing.

A stack of letters

"The Need to Say It" continued

I handed over the paper for her to sign. She always asked if her signature looked nice. She wrote her one word—Teresa—with a <u>flourish</u>. For her, writing was painting, a visual art, not <u>declarative</u> but <u>sensuous</u>.

She sent her <u>lean</u> documents regularly to her only remaining sister who lived in Los Angeles, a place she had not visited. They had last seen each other as children in their village in <u>Bohemia</u>. But she never mentioned that or anything from that world. There was no taint of <u>reminiscence</u> in her <u>prose</u>.

Even at ten I was <u>appalled</u> by the <u>minimalism</u> of these letters. They enraged me. "Is that all you have to say?" I would ask her, a nasty edge to my voice.

STOP AND PREDICT

What do you predict Patricia will begin doing with the letters?

....

....

....

....

It wasn't long before I began <u>padding</u> the text. Without telling her, I added an <u>anecdote</u> my father had told at dinner the night before, or I conducted this unknown reader through the heavy plot of my brother's attempt to make <u>first string</u> on the St. Thomas hockey team. I allowed myself a descriptive <u>aria</u> on the beauty of Minnesota winters (for the benefit of my California

VOCABULARY

flourish—dramatic style.
declarative—serving to declare or state.
sensuous—pleasing to the senses.
lean—thin.
Bohemia—region of the Czech Republic.
reminiscence—remembering the past.
prose—writing.
appalled—upset.
minimalism—simplicity; use of the barest essentials.
padding—adding to.
anecdote—interesting short story.
first string—a starting position.
aria—lovely vocal piece in an opera.

A young woman with her grandmother

reader who might need some background material on the subject of ice hockey). A little of this, a little of that—there was always something I could toss into my grandmother's <u>meager</u> soup to thicken it up.

Of course the protagonist of the hockey tale was not "my brother." He was "my grandson." I departed from my own life without a regret and breezily inhabited my grandmother's.

I complained about my hip joint, I <u>bemoaned</u> the rising cost of hamburger, I even touched on the loneliness of old age, and hinted at the inattention of my son's wife (that is, my own mother, who was next door, <u>oblivious</u> to <u>treachery</u>).

In time, my grandmother gave in to the inevitable. Without ever discussing it, we understood that when she came looking for me, clicking her ball-point, I was to write the letter, and her job was to keep the cookies coming. I abandoned her <u>skimpy floral stationery</u>, which badly cramped my style, and thumped down on the table a tack of <u>ruled 8½ x 11</u>.

"Just say something interesting," she would say. And I was off to the races.

What does she mean that her "grandmother gave in to the inevitable"?

VOCABULARY
meager—weak; lean.
bemoaned—expressed sadness about.
oblivious—unaware.
treachery—betrayal.
skimpy floral stationery—thin, frilly, and flowery writing paper.
ruled 8 1/2 x 11—lined paper that is 8 1/2 inches wide and 11 inches long.

"The Need to Say It" continued

I took over her life in prose. Somewhere along the line, though, she decided to take full possession of her sign-off. She asked me to show her how to write "Love" so she could add it to "Teresa" in her own hand. She practiced the new word many times on scratch paper before she allowed herself to commit it to the bottom of a letter.

But when she finally took the leap, I realized I had forgotten to tell her about the comma. On a single slanting line she had written: *Love Teresa*. The words didn't look like a closure, but a command.

Write about what you know. This instruction from grade school was the first bit of writing advice I was ever given. Terrific—that was just what I wanted to do. But privately, in a <u>recess</u> of my personality I could not gain access to by wish or by will, I was afraid this advice was a lie, <u>concocted</u> and <u>disseminated</u> nationwide by English teachers. The real, the secret, <u>commandment</u> was *Write about what matters.*

■ VOCABULARY ■
recess—secret, remote part.
concocted—created.
disseminated—spread.
commandment—rule.

STOP AND SUMMARIZE STOP AND SUMMARIZE

Describe what this essay is about in a few sentences.

....

....

....

....

....

....

....

....

GATHER YOUR THOUGHTS

A. MAKE INFERENCES An inference is information found out by reasoning and making good guesses. Based on this article, what inferences can you make about Patricia Hampl? Make some notes on the diagram below.

HOW GRANDMA SEES HER

WHAT I THINK SHE'S LIKE

Patricia Hampl

WHAT I THINK ABOUT HER

HOW SHE SEES THINGS

WHAT THINGS SHE SAYS

B. DEVELOP AN OPINION Think about what Patricia Hampl did in adding details to the letters she helped her grandmother write.

1. Get ready to write a paragraph of opinion by answering the question: "How do you feel about what Patricia Hampl did?"

MY OPINION

2. List 3 reasons or examples that would help someone understand why you feel the way you do.

1.

2.

3.

IV. WRITE

Write a **paragraph of opinion** that explains how you feel about what Patricia Hampl did.

1. Begin with a topic sentence that clearly states your opinion.
2. Include at least 2 reasons or examples that explain why you feel the way you do.
3. End with a concluding sentence that restates your opinion.
4. Use the Writers' Checklist to revise your paragraph.

WRITERS' CHECKLIST

USAGE PROBLEMS

☐ Did you avoid problems with *who's* and *whose*? *Who's* is the contraction for *who is*. *Whose* is a possessive pronoun, one which shows ownership. EXAMPLES: *Who's responsible for this mess? Can we decide whose lunch bag was left to spoil?*

☐ Did you use *principle* and *principal* correctly? Use *principal* to mean main. *Principle* means a general rule. EXAMPLES: *My principal source of amusement is going to movies. The principle of telling the truth is important to my grandparents.*

V. WRAP-UP

What did you like or not like about Hampl's writing style?

READERS' CHECKLIST

STYLE

- ❑ Did you find the passage well written?
- ❑ Are the sentences well constructed and the words well chosen?
- ❑ Does the style show you how to be a better writer?

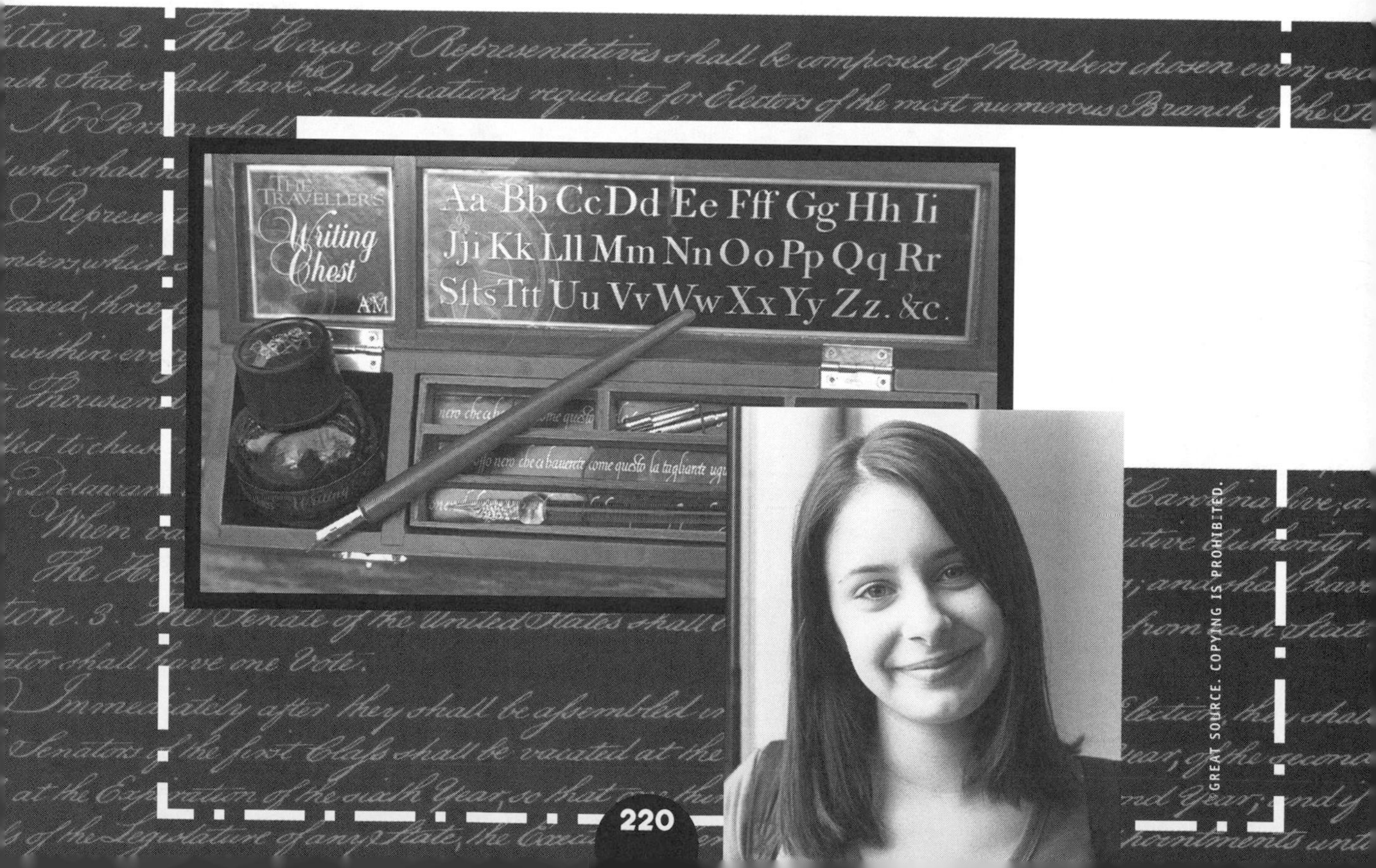

THE TRAVELLER'S Writing Chest
AM
Aa Bb CcDd Ee Fff Gg Hh Ii
Jji Kk Lll Mm Nn Oo Pp Qq Rr
Sfts Ttt Uu Vv Ww Xx Yy Zz. &c.

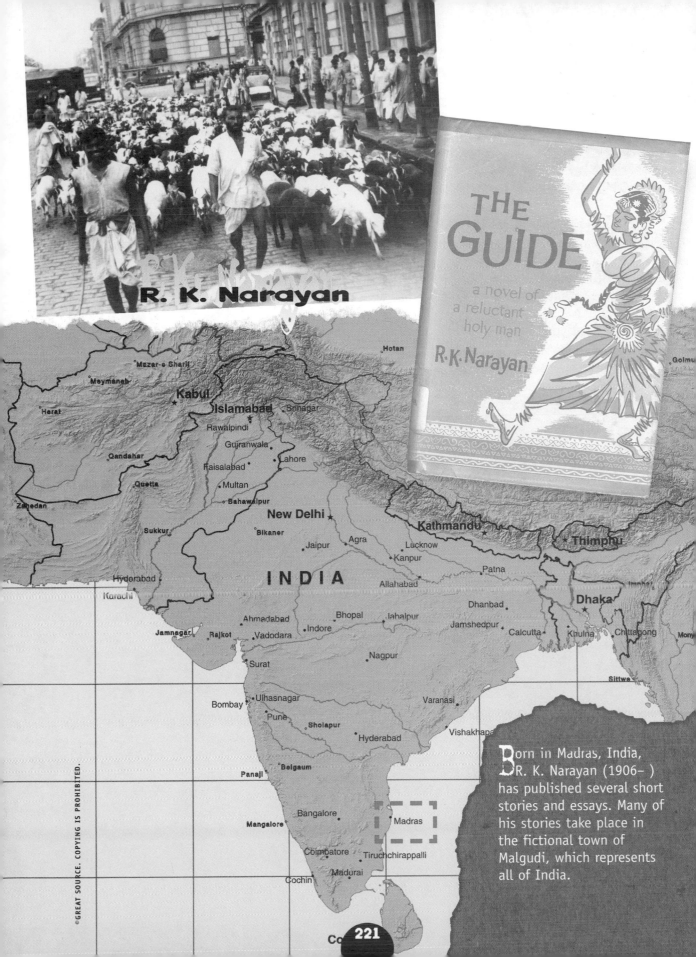

R. K. Narayan

THE GUIDE
a novel of a reluctant holy man
R. K. Narayan

Born in Madras, India, R. K. Narayan (1906–) has published several short stories and essays. Many of his stories take place in the fictional town of Malgudi, which represents all of India.

Did you ever invent imaginary friends or places? R. K. Narayan's novels present a whole imaginary town called Malgudi. His works are known for their amusing characters and gentle humor.

BEFORE YOU READ

R.K. Narayan's novel *The Guide* begins with the story of Raju, a character who has a fresh start in life.

1. Think about the phrase *a fresh start*. What does it mean to you? What feelings, experiences, people, or places come to mind?

2. Record your ideas about what *fresh start* means on the Word Web below.

WORD WEB

fresh start

READ

Read at your own pace.

1. As you read, think about what Raju is like.

2. Try to **clarify** Raju's character by making notes in the Response Notes.

"Raju" from *The Guide* by R. K. Narayan

RESPONSE NOTES

Raju welcomed the intrusion—something to relieve the loneliness of the place. The man stood gazing <u>reverentially</u> on his face. Raju felt amused and embarrassed. "Sit down if you like," Raju said, to break the spell. The other accepted the suggestion with a grateful nod and went down the river steps to wash his feet and face, came up wiping himself dry with the end of a checkered yellow towel on his shoulder, and took his seat two steps below the <u>granite</u> slab on which Raju was sitting crosslegged as if it were a throne, beside an ancient <u>shrine</u>. The branches of the trees <u>canopying</u> the river course rustled and trembled with the <u>agitation</u> of birds and monkeys settling down for the night. Upstream beyond the hills the sun was setting. Raju waited for the other to say something. But he was too polite to open a conversation.

Raju asked, "Where are you from?" dreading lest the other should turn around and ask the same question.

The man replied, "I'm from Mangal—"

"Where is Mangal?"

The other waved his arm, indicating a direction across the river, beyond the high steep bank. "Not far from here," he added. The man volunteered further information about himself. "My daughter lives nearby. I

EXAMPLE:
Raju seems to like meeting and talking with people.

VOCABULARY

reverentially—in awe; respectfully.
granite—hard, coarse-grained rock.
shrine—site of devotion and worship.
canopying—arching so as to cover.
agitation—movement.

had gone to visit her; I am now on my way home. I left her after food. She insisted that I should stay on to dinner, but I refused. It'd have meant walking home at nearly midnight. I'm not afraid of anything, but why should we walk when we ought to be sleeping in bed?"

"You are very sensible," Raju said.

They listened for a while to the chatter of monkeys, and the man added as an afterthought, "My daughter is married to my own sister's son, and so there is no problem. I often visit my sister and also my daughter; and so no one minds it."

"Why should anyone mind in any case if you visit a daughter?"

"It's not considered proper form to pay too many visits to a son-in-law," explained the villager.

Storyboard

1. How does the story begin?

2. What do you learn about the man from Mangal?

3. What do you learn about Raju?

"Raju" CONTINUED

Raju liked this <u>rambling</u> talk. He had been all alone in this place for over a day. It was good to hear the human voice again. After this the villager resumed the study of his face with intense respect. And Raju stroked his chin thoughtfully to make sure that an <u>apostolic beard</u> had not suddenly grown there. It was still smooth. He had had his last shave only two days before and paid for it with the hard earned coins of his jail life.

<u>Loquacious</u> as usual and with the sharp blade scraping the soap, the barber had asked, "Coming out, I suppose?" Raju rolled his eyes and remained silent. He felt <u>irritated</u> at the question, but did not like to show it with the fellow holding the knife. "Just coming out?" repeated the barber <u>obstinately</u>.

Raju felt it would be no use being angry with such a man. Here he was in the presence of experience. He asked, "How do you know?"

VOCABULARY
rambling—easygoing; aimless.
apostolic beard—beard resembling one worn by Jesus's disciples.
Loquacious—talkative.
irritated—annoyed.
obstinately—stubbornly.

RESPONSE NOTES

"I have spent twenty years shaving people here. Didn't you observe that this was the first shop as you left the jail gate? Half the trick is to have your business in the right place. But that raises other people's jealousies!" he said, waving off an army of jealous barbers."

"Don't you attend to the inmates?"

"Not until they come out. It is my brother's son who is on duty there. I don't want to compete with him and I don't want to enter the jail gates every day."

"Not a bad place," said Raju through the soap.

"Go back then," said the barber and asked, "What was it? What did the police say?"

"Don't talk of it," snapped Raju and tried to maintain a <u>sullen</u>, <u>forbidding</u> silence for the rest of the shave.

Storyboard

4. What does the barber help us learn about Raju?

5. What do we learn about the barber?

VOCABULARY
sullen—gloomy.
forbidding—unpleasant.

III. GATHER YOUR THOUGHTS

A. ANALYZE A CHARACTER Use the organizer below to help you review what you know about the character of Raju.

2. What is Raju like with the barber?

1. What is Raju like with the man from Mangal?

Raju

3. What is Raju like from what he says?

B. PLAN A PARAGRAPH Prepare to write a character sketch of Raju.
1. Write your overall impression of him in the topic sentence.
2. Then write 3 words to describe him. Beneath each word, write details from the story that support your idea.
3. Add a concluding sentence that restates your impression of the character.

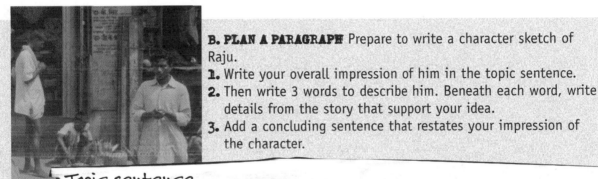

Topic sentence

Conclusion

Now write a **character sketch** to describe Raju.

1. Use your planning from the previous page to organize your paragraph about Raju.
2. Begin with a topic sentence to give your overall impression.
3. Then explain 3 characteristics of Raju by presenting evidence from the story to support your opinion of him.
4. End with a concluding sentence restating your impression.
5. Use the Writers' Checklist to help you revise.

WRITERS' CHECKLIST

USAGE

☐ Did you use *good, better,* and *best* correctly?
Better is the comparative form of *good.* Use *better* when you are comparing two things. *Best* is the superlative form of *good.* Use *best* when you are comparing more than two things. EXAMPLES: *Being free is better than being in jail. Freedom is best of all.*

☐ Did you use *bad, worse,* and *worst* correctly?
Worse is the comparative form of *bad.* Use *worse* when you are comparing two things. *Worst* is the superlative form of *bad.* Use *worst* when you are comparing more than two things. EXAMPLES: *Jail was worse than being free. The waiting to get out was the worst feeling of all.*

V. WRAP-UP

How do you like the story so far? Would you recommend it to a friend?

READERS' CHECKLIST

ENJOYMENT

☐ Did you like the reading?
☐ Was the reading experience pleasurable?
☐ Would you want to reread the piece or recommend it to someone?

Do people you know change depending on who they are with? Around friends a person may act one way, and around a parent or older brother or sister the same person may seem wholly different. People reveal different sides of themselves at different times and in different settings.

BEFORE YOU READ

With a partner, take turns reading the sentences below that are taken from the story. Think about the different sides of Raju that are revealed.

1. Put the number 1 next to the sentence you think comes first in the story, 2 beside the sentence that comes next, and so on.

2. Then try to answer the questions below and share your responses with other groups.

THINK-PAIR-AND-SHARE

_____ "If you are lucky enough to be guided by Raju, you will know everything."

_____ "It's written on your face that you are a two-year sort, which means you are not a murderer."

_____ "I should have grown up like a thousand other normal persons, without worries in life."

_____ "I am here because I have nowhere else to go. I want to be away from people who may recognize me."

What new information did you learn about Raju?

....

....

What do you predict will happen to Raju?

....

....

READ
Now read the rest of the episode about Raju.
1. **Mark** or **highlight** information about your predictions on the previous page.
2. Note any parts of the story that you especially like in the Response Notes.

"Raju" (continued) from *The Guide* by R. K. Narayan

But the barber was not to be <u>cowed</u> so easily. His lifelong contact with tough men had hardened him. He said, "Eighteen months or twenty-four? I can bet it's one or the other."

Raju felt admiration for the man. He was a master. It was no use losing one's temper. "You are so wise and knowing. Why do you ask questions?"

The barber was pleased with the compliment. His fingers paused in their operations; he bent round to face Raju and say, "Just to get it out of you, that is all. It's written on your face that you are a two-year sort, which means you are not a murderer."

"How can you tell?" Raju said.

"You would look different if you had been in for seven years, which is what one gets for murder only half-proved."

"What else have I not done?" Raju asked.

"You have not cheated in any big way; but perhaps only in a small, <u>petty</u> manner."

"Go on. What next?"

"You have not <u>abducted</u> or raped anyone, or set fire to a house."

"Why don't you say exactly why I was sent to jail for two years? I'll give you four <u>annas</u> for a guess."

EXAMPLE:
I like the way the barber keeps drawing conclusions about Raju.

VOCABULARY
cowed—frightened; made afraid.
petty—unimportant; trivial.
abducted—kidnapped.
annas—Arabian currency.

STOP AND PREDICT

What do you think will happen next to Raju? What makes you think so?

_____

_____

_____

_____

_____

RESPONSE NOTES

"Raju" CONTINUED

"No time now for a game," said the barber and went on, "What do you do next?"

"I don't know. Must go somewhere, I suppose," said Raju thoughtfully.

"In case you like to go back to your old company, why don't you put your hand in someone's pocket at the market, or walk through an open door and pick out some trash and let the people howl for the police? They'll see you back where you want to be."

"Not a bad place," Raju repeated, slightly nodding in the direction of the jail wall. "Friendly people there—but I hate to be awakened every morning at five."

"An hour at which a <u>night-prowler</u> likes to return home to bed, I suppose," said the barber with heavy <u>insinuation</u>. "Well, that's all. You may get up," he said, putting away the razor. "You look like a <u>maharaja</u> now"—surveying Raju at a distance from his chair.

The villager on the lower step looked up at his face with devotion, which <u>irked</u> Raju. "Why do you look at me like that?" he asked <u>brusquely</u>.

VOCABULARY
night-prowler—person who roams in search of prey.
insinuation—suggestion.
maharaja—prince in India.
irked—annoyed.
brusquely—discourteously; roughly.

"Raju" CONTINUED

The man replied, "I don't know. I don't mean to offend you, sir." Raju wanted to blurt out. "I am here because I have nowhere else to go. I want to be away from people who may recognize me." But he hesitated, wondering how he should say it. It looked as though he would be hurting the other's deepest sentiment if he so much as whispered the word "jail." He tried at least to say, "I am not so great as you imagine. I am just ordinary." Before he could fumble and reach the words, the other said, "I have a problem, sir."

"Tell me about it," Raju said, the old, old habit of <u>affording</u> guidance to others <u>asserting</u> itself. Tourists who recommended him to one another would say at one time, "If you are lucky enough to be guided by Raju, you will know everything. He will not only show you all the worth-while places, but also help you in every way." It was in his nature to get involved in other people's interests and activities. "Otherwise," Raju often reflected, "I should have grown up like a thousand other normal persons, without worries in life."

VOCABULARY
affording—giving; providing.
asserting—declaring; expressing.

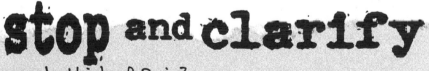

stop and clarify

What do other people think of Raju?

_____

_____

What is Raju really like?

_____

_____

_____

A. FORM AN OPINION Suppose you had to write a review of "Raju."

1. Develop your opinion about "Raju" by considering the plot, characters, setting, theme, and writing style.
2. After you've finished, compare your responses with a partner and discuss why you agree or disagree.

DIRECTIONS: Rate "Raju," the first chapter from *The Guide*. Circle the rating you think is most appropriate for each aspect of the story.

THE CHARACTERS ARE...

1	2	3	4	5	6	7	8	9	10

very interesting   kind of interesting   not at all interesting

THE PLOT IS...

1	2	3	4	5	6	7	8	9	10

very interesting   kind of interesting   not at all interesting

THE SETTING IS...

1	2	3	4	5	6	7	8	9	10

very interesting   kind of interesting   not at all interesting

THE DIALOGUE IS...

1	2	3	4	5	6	7	8	9	10

very interesting   kind of interesting   not at all interesting

THE THEME IS...

1	2	3	4	5	6	7	8	9	10

very interesting   kind of interesting   not at all interesting

THE WRITING IS...

1	2	3	4	5	6	7	8	9	10

very interesting   kind of interesting   not at all interesting

B. BUILD A REVIEW To write a good review, you will need to support your opinion. You will also need to present a balanced view, suggesting what you liked most and what you like least.

1. Fill out the graphic below by first writing what you liked most about the story of Raju.

2. Then find a part of the story—a sentence or some dialogue—that supports your opinion.

3. Then do the same for what you liked least about the story.

What I liked most

What I liked least

Support from the story

Support from the story

C. DRAFT A TOPIC SENTENCE Now write a sentence that gives your overall opinion of the story.

1. Draft your topic sentence for a review you will write of "Raju."

2. Revise it until it contains all of the following:

☑ name of author and title of story
☑ clear, brief statement of your opinion
☑ catchy beginning to get the reader's interest

IV. WRITE

Now write a **review** of Raju's story.

1. Begin with your topic sentence from the previous page.

2. Then tell what you liked most and least about the story, giving evidence from the story for each part.

3. Finish with a concluding sentence that sums up your overall opinion.

4. Use the Writers' Checklist to help you revise.

> topic sentence
>
> part you liked most
>
> part you liked least
>
> conclusion

WRITERS' CHECKLIST

CAPITALIZATION AND PUNCTUATION

❑ **Do all of the sentences start with a capital letter?**

❑ **Do all of the sentences end with an end punctuation mark?**
EXAMPLE: *The character of Raju is fascinating.*

❑ **Did you underline book titles and use quotation marks around story or chapter titles?** EXAMPLES: *The novel is The Guide by R. K. Narayan. "Raju" is a frustrating story.*

V. WRAP-UP

How easy or difficult to read was Narayan's story?

READERS' CHECKLIST

EASE

☐ Was the passage easy to read?

☐ Were you able to read it smoothly and without difficulty?

Acknowledgments

41 "The Land" from *Cry, the Beloved Country* by Alan Paton. Reprinted with the permission of Scribner, a Division of Simon & Schuster, Inc. from CRY, THE BELOVED COUNTRY by Alan Paton. Copyright 1948 by Charles Scribner's Sons; copyright renewed © 1976 by Hannah Tillich.

51, 60 "Okonkwo's Story" from THINGS FALL APART by Chinua Achebe. © 1958 Chinua Achebe. Reprinted by permission of Heinemann Educational Publishers, a division of Reed Educational & Professional Publishing, Ltd.

71 Letter and diary of Barbara Pym from A VERY PRIVATE EYE by Barbara Pym. Copyright © 1984 by Hilary Walton. Preface and all editorial text © by Hazel Holt. Used by permission of Dutton, a division of Penguin Putnam Inc.

89 "The Gray Beginnings" by Rachel Carson from THE SEA AROUND US by Rachel Carson. Copyright 1950, 1951, 1961 by Rachel Carson renewed 1979 by Roger Christie. Used by permission of Oxford University Press, Inc.

113, 120 "The Death of the Moth" by Virginia Woolf from THE DEATH OF THE MOTH AND OTHER ESSAYS by Virginia Woolf. Copyright 1942 by Harcourt, Inc. and renewed 1970 by Marjorie T. Parsons, Executrix. Reprinted by permission of the publisher.

129 "Death in the Sun" Peter Kumalo for "Death in the Sun," published in Drum.

149 "Stuck Fast" from SOUTH by Ernest Shackleton. Reprinted by special arrangement with The Lyons Press.

158 "One Way Out" from ENDURANCE *by* Alfred Lansing. Reprinted by permission of Carroll & Graf Publishers, inc.

169, 178 "The Brilliant Konrad Schneider" from *Childhood's End* by Arthur C. Clarke. Reprinted by permission of the author and the author's agents, Scovil Chichak Galen Literary Agency, Inc.

189 "Father" by J. M. Coetzee from BOYHOOD: SCENES FROM A PROVINCIAL LIFE by J. M. Coetzee, Copyright © 1997 by J. M. Coetzee. Used by permission of Viking Penguin, a division of Penguin Putnam Inc.

196 "Mama Is Chinese" from LEAVES FROM THE MENTAL PORTFOLIO OF AN EURASIAN by Sui Sin Far (Edith Maud Eton). Reprinted from THE OXFORD BOOK OF WOMEN'S WRITING IN THE UNITED STATES, edited by Linda Wagner-Martin and Cathy N. Davidson.

205 "14 December 1959" from LETTERS OF C. S. LEWIS. Copyright © 1966 by W. H. Lewis and the Executors of C. S. Lewis and renewed 1994 by C. S. Lewis PTE Ltd. Reprinted by permission of Harcourt, Inc.

212 "The Need to Say It" by Patricia Hampl © 1991 by Patricia Hampl. Originally published in THE WRITER AND HER WORK, Janet Sternberg, ed., published by W. W. Norton. Permission granted by Rhonda Weyr Agency, NY.

223, 231 "Raju" by R. K. Narayan from THE GUIDE. Copyright © 1958 by R. K. Narayan. Published by Penguin Books. Permission granted by the Wallace Literary Agency.

Photography

COVER: All photos © Eileen Ryan.

TABLE OF CONTENTS and INTRODUCTION: Page 3: courtesy Library of Congress. Page 4: all photos ©Eileen Ryan. Page 5: All photos ©Eileen Ryan except upper right, left center—courtesy Library of Congress and upper center—courtesy NASA. Pages 6–8: all photos ©Eileen Ryan. Page 9: all photos courtesy Library of Congress. Page 10: all photos ©Eileen Ryan.

CHAPTER 1: All photos courtesy Library of Congress except where noted. Page 11: top and lower right—©Eileen Ryan. Pages 14, 19-20—©Eileen Ryan. Page 21: upper left—©Eileen Ryan. Page 28—©Eileen Ryan. Page 30: background—©Eileen Ryan.

CHAPTER 2: All photos © Eileen Ryan except where noted. Page 31: top inset, lower left—courtesy Library of Congress. Page 35: lower right—courtesy Library of Congress. Page 39: inset—courtesy Library of Congress. Pages 40-42, 44: courtesy Library of Congress. Page 45: top—courtesy Library of Congress. Page 48: lower left—courtesy Library of Congress.

CHAPTER 3: All photos courtesy Library of Congress except where noted. Pages 52, 55, 61, 67: background—© Eileen Ryan.

CHAPTER 4: All photos © Eileen Ryan except where noted. Page 69: lower right—courtesy Library of Congress. Page 70: upper right—courtesy Library of Congress. Page 71: lower right—Photodisc. Page 72: Superstock. Page 73: Photodisc. Page 75: Photodisc. Page 77: courtesy Library of Congress. Page 79: inset—Photodisc. Page 80: upper right—courtesy Library of Congress. Page 86: right—courtesy Library of Congress.

CHAPTER 5: All photos © Eileen Ryan except where noted. Page 87: NASA, except author photos, bottom—courtesy Library of Congress, Page 89: bottom—NASA, Page 91: lower right—NASA. Page 92: NASA. Page 93: lower right—NASA. Page 94: NASA. Page 97: inset—NASA. Page 98, 100: inset—courtesy Library of Congress. Page 103: courtesy Library of Congress. Page 106: inset—courtesy Library of Congress. Page 108: upper right—courtesy Library of Congress.

CHAPTER 6: All photos courtesy Library of Congress except where noted. Page 111: center left—©Eileen Ryan. Page 113: upper left—©Eileen Ryan. Page 117: background—©Eileen Ryan.

CHAPTER 7: All photos courtesy Library of Congress except where noted. Page 128: background—©Eileen Ryan. Page 129: ©Eileen Ryan. Page 131-2, 136-7: background—©Eileen Ryan. Page 138: background, lower left—©Eileen Ryan.

CHAPTER 8: All photos courtesy Library of Congress except where noted. Page 149: upper left—©Eileen Ryan. Page 155, 164,165: ©Eileen Ryan.

CHAPTER 9: All photos courtesy NASA except where noted. Page 167: upper right—courtesy Library of Congress. Page 168-9: background—©Eileen Ryan. Page 170: bottom—©Eileen Ryan.

CHAPTER 10: All photos ©Eileen Ryan except where noted. Page 188: top—courtesy Library of Congress. Page 189, 193: courtesy Library of Congress. Page 195: lower left—courtesy Library of Congress.

CHAPTER 11: All photos © Eileen Ryan except where noted. Page 203: top center—courtesy Library of Congress. Page 212: inset—courtesy Library of Congress. Page 214: Photodisc. Page 215: Photodisc.

CHAPTER 12: All photos courtesy Library of Congress except where noted. Page 226: ©Eileen Ryan.

Cover and Book Design: Christine Ronan and Sean O'Neill, Ronan Design

Permissions:
Feldman and Associates

Developed by Nieman Inc.

The editors have made every effort to trace the ownership of all copyrighted selections found in this book and to make full acknowledgment for their use. Omissions brought to our attention will be corrected in a subsequent edition.

Author/Title Index